Running Naked Down the Road

A Memoir

It's not about running or being naked

Bettie Wailes

Other books by Bettie Wailes

Running in the Back of the Pack

SAT Grammar—Prioritized

Contributor to:

Chicken Soup for the Soul: Runners
Chicken Soup for the Soul: Grandmothers
Chicken Soup for the Soul: Grieving and Recovery

Running Naked Down the Road

A Memoir

Bettie Wailes

Running Naked Down the Road

Wise Owl Publishing
2914 Banchory Road
Winter Park, FL 32792

Copyright © 2018, Bettie Wailes

All rights reserved. No part of this work may be reproduced or transmitted in any form, or by any means, electronic or mechanical, without written permission from the publisher. Exceptions are made for brief excerpts to be used in published reviews.

ISBN: 978-1-938464-05-8

Dedication

I dedicate this work to my daughters, Karen and Linda. Without their understanding and help, I never could have completed my degree. They shouldered responsibilities at ages too young, endured meager circumstances, and kept me focused when I wanted to give up. I hope they know their sacrifices contributed to a better future for all of us.

I love you, my sweet girls.

Acknowledgments

Once again, I cannot express enough gratitude for my writing group—Doug, Teresa, Nylda, and Liz. Without you, this would still be collecting virtual dust. Thank you, Nylda, for the exclamations points! And thank you, Teresa, for removing some of them. Doug, I'm grateful to you for keeping the direction of the quotes straight. Liz, thank you for deleting unnecessary words.

Also, I thank my sweet Jimmy for listening patiently to boring descriptions of the writing and editing process. You encouraged me when I needed it. Most of all, you loved me every day. Thank you for your constant support. I love you head to toe, front to back, inside and out, forever and ever.

You're never given a dream without also being given the power to make it true.

You might have to work for it, however.

--Richard Bach,
author of *Jonathan Livingston Seagull*

Chapter 1

I thought I was safe

March 1969

Knock-knock.
Shucks! I hate being interrupted.
Annoyed, I banged out one last chord and rose, pushing back the piano bench.

I didn't need to see his face to know the long, lean silhouette at the back door belonged to Richard.

What's he doing here? He was just here to pick up the girls. I hope nothing's wrong.

Pulling back the green gingham curtain covering the glass in the back door, I studied his steady, upright stance. His blue eyes were clear, and he wore that same smile that years earlier had reminded me of country singer Jimmy Dean. Even after all that had happened since, I remembered how that smile had captured my attention, eventually causing me to give him my heart.

"Hi, Bet. Can I come in?" He had changed into fresh clothes, his wavy brown hair was neat, and his speech was clear.

I looked up into his face.

He's definitely sober.

It wouldn't have been unusual for him to be drinking at four o'clock on a Sunday afternoon, but I'd just seen him less than two hours before when he'd come to get our two daughters to take them to his mother's for a visit.

So without knowing why, I opened the door only a crack. "What are you doing here again?"

"I just wanna talk to you. It's important."

Maybe he just wants to get more of his things.

I cautiously eased the door open. Six week before, when I filed for divorce, I had asked him to move out. He had taken only a few things to his mother's, saying he would stay there temporarily.

We'll see how temporary, I had thought.

He had agreed when I insisted we be civil to each other—no fighting or using the children as pawns.

Surely he's not here to talk about the divorce.

Standing in the center of the square kitchen, Richard fidgeted, shifting his weight first to one leg and then the other, his thumbs stuck through his belt loops. I remained standing, too, to indicate that I expected his visit to be brief.

"How's your car?" He tilted his head toward the two-year-old '67 VW Beetle sitting in the carport. I had bought it just two weeks earlier with a loan from my mother.

"Fine."

He didn't come here to talk about my car. And why is he so nervous?

In a flash, he drew himself up to his full six-foot-two height as his expression changed from a smile to a frown, as if steeling for a purpose. "I came to take you for a drive."

"A drive?"

"Yeah. We're gonna take a ride. Let's go."

"Whatever you have to say, you can say it right here." A knot formed in my stomach—not quite fear, but close.

"You don't understand." The frown deepened, his face grew taut, and the muscles in his jaws tightened. "I'm not askin', I'm tellin'. Now come on."

I didn't have time to process his mood shift before, in one swift motion, he grabbed my left arm, twisted it behind my back, and pinned me next to him. The needle on my fear meter now jumped into the red zone.

Why is he so angry? Where is he taking me?

I forced myself to push aside the questions, knowing I must stay calm.

If he had been drinking, I would have expected him to start with his usual accusation, "You think you're Little Miss Perfect, don't you? You must think you're Jesus H. Christ hisself. What makes you think you're so perfect?"

Early on, I had learned that there was no satisfactory answer. When I tried to defend myself against his anger, he easily overpowered my five-foot-two, one-hundred-five-pound frame. He didn't fight so violently as to injure me beyond a few bruises, but on one occasion he retaliated by taking our two-year old daughter away in the middle of the night. So I learned to grit my teeth and endure his attentions. One of the reasons I had been driven to divorce was the fear of his violence escalating.

But today was different. I simply had no experience with him both sober and hostile.

He steered me out the door using the arm he held firmly behind my back. In spite of past experience, once outside I screamed as loudly as I could, desperately hoping someone would hear and come to help. The neighbors around us knew all too well about Richard, but would they be willing to get involved?

Richard jerked my arm higher up my back, and put his other hand over my mouth as he forced me toward his truck. He warned, "Don't scream again or I'm gonna break your arm. Understand?"

To underline the threat, he jerked my arm hard enough to cause the ache in my shoulder to sharpen. I caught my breath and gritted my teeth. I should have known the futility of resisting.

Ouch!

I nodded my agreement as I fought back tears, but I couldn't help wondering what he intended to do. Urgent pain shot through my shoulder.

I need to find a way to get away from him.

Detachment pushed aside the throbbing—something I had learned to do during earlier episodes with Richard. I had learned to stay in my head, only allowing myself to give in to the emotions after the crisis was over.

Removing one hand from my mouth to open the truck door, Richard pushed me in on the driver's side, and shoved me across the bench seat as he slid in after me. He awkwardly reached around the steering wheel with his left hand to start the truck, maintaining his grip on my arm with his right hand.

The frown remained set and the muscles in his jaws continued to twitch as he drove out of the neighborhood and headed north. After a few miles, he pulled into a service station that had a couple of pay phones at the edge of the parking lot. He turned and sneered, "You know what I'm gonna do? I'm gonna make you strip nekkid, and then take pictures of you. I'm gonna degrade you like you've degraded me. What do you think about that? We'll see how perfect you are then." Spittle accompanied his words.

Then he added, "But first I need to make a phone call."

For an instant, I wondered how he thought I had degraded him, but quickly decided that question could wait. I needed to escape his irrational rage. The last thing I wanted was to end up in a deserted place with him this angry. More than likely, he had at least one gun with him, and he had threatened me before.

I frantically looked around for help. My eyes locked on several men about fifty feet away who stood facing away from us. Still holding my arm behind my back, Richard forced me with him to a pay phone. He fumbled in his pocket for coins and then dialed. In a controlled voice he said, "Mom, I'm out here at the Billups Station on 61 North. I need you to bring me the Polaroid camera."

I leaned toward the phone and screamed, "Help, Rita!" hoping to alert my mother-in-law that Richard was once again "on a tear," as she called it.

Richard slammed the receiver onto its hook. Through clenched teeth, he said, "See what you made me do? Now I'll have to change the plan."

Desperate for some way to avoid getting back into the truck with him, I yelled toward the group of men. "Help! Call the police. Please help!"

A couple of the men glanced our way briefly, but then shrugged and returned to their conversation.

Please, can't you see I'm in trouble?

Richard forced me back into the truck, and drove north again. His eyes darted alternately to either side of the highway and to me, the muscles in his jaws still working furiously. I could almost see his brain muddled with what to do next. After a couple of miles, he glanced at the gas gauge and abruptly pulled into another gas station.

The station had both self-service and full-service pumps. I was certain he didn't want to get out of the car and leave me unrestrained. As I expected, Richard chose the full-service island on the left. I mouthed "help" over Richard's shoulder to the attendant, but he was very young—and oblivious.

Meanwhile, a couple I recognized from a college night class had driven up to the self-service island to our right, heading south, the opposite direction from us. They didn't understand what I was mouthing to them, but curiosity kept them looking.

When the attendant returned for payment, Richard was forced to release my arm to get money from his pocket. At that moment, I scrambled out of the truck and into the couple's car, pleading, "Please take me with you, and hurry! Richard's crazy and he's threatening me. I don't know what he'll do next."

They hesitated for the split second it took to look over at Richard. They barely knew me and didn't know him at all.

Afraid to look back at Richard, I kept pleading, "Please help me. I'm afraid he might kill me!"

The wife turned around and looked at me, and instinctively reached back and took my hand, then looked at her husband. Her silent communication worked. He drove away, saying they would take me only a short distance. Since I had just told them Richard was crazy, the husband was understandably afraid of what Richard might do.

My eyes searched for a safe place. I spotted the truck weigh station just ahead. I hoped Richard wouldn't think to look there, but if he did, there was a good chance a state trooper would be there to offer protection.

The car stopped barely long enough for me to get out and then sped away. I ran inside. The only person there was the attendant, an older gentleman, who looked up and smiled.

Darn! No trooper!

As I was explaining why I wanted to use the phone, I realized I had no money—not even a dime for a pay phone. The desperation on my face must have been convincing, because he offered me the regular phone.

I called Clarice, who lived directly across the street. My mother lived too far away. Besides, I was reluctant to tell her about most of these episodes, much less ask her to get involved. Rita, my mother-in-law, was already busy with the girls. Clarice was the only other person whose phone number I knew and who I hoped would understand.

By now, the attendant's face was a combination of curiosity and pity, but he didn't ask any questions. I had never wished so hard to become invisible, not only to the attendant, but also to Richard if he should figure out where I was. My eyes searched every vehicle that passed, finally locking onto Clarice's blue Oldsmobile.

During the drive back to the neighborhood, I shivered as I explained what had happened. She wasn't shocked; she had watched as the police had been called to our house. We decided it was unsafe for me to return to my own house. She suggested I stay in her house, hoping Richard wouldn't find me there. Clarice would go next door to rejoin the card game with her husband and the neighboring couple. My phone call had no doubt interrupted an intense Bridge match.

Darkness had fallen by the time we arrived, so I slipped into Clarice's unlighted house as she went to the neighbors'. In the stillness, I considered Richard's hostility.

What could have set him off? What will he try next?

I tried to calm down, but my heart raced.

Should I call the police? What would I report? He hasn't actually done anything illegal. Not yet anyway.

I knew from past incidents that the police were reluctant to get involved, usually making excuses for Richard and downplaying his behavior. In 1969 in Natchez, Mississippi, the good ol' boy attitude was alive and well.

Waiting and listening, I flinched at every sound, but mostly heard my own heartbeat throbbing in my ears. Eventually, I relaxed a little, trying to believe he had given up on his mission, whatever it had been.

About eight-thirty, with everything quiet, I decided to go across the street to my house. But the sound of a vehicle driving slowly into the alley behind Clarice's house caused me to halt my half-crouched walk before I reached the front door. It sounded like it stopped directly behind the house. Curious who would be in the alley on a Sunday evening, I crept to the back of her house, carefully remaining in shadows.

It's Richard!

He rolled down the window, brought up a rifle, and pointed it at Clarice's house.

How did he find me? Is he going to kill me?

Panic worse than before set in. I prayed, *Dear God, please help me! What do I do now?*

Like melting Jell-O, my body drained to the floor. A maelstrom of images darted around in my head. Several seconds passed before lucid thoughts began to form.

Now it's time to call the police!

I crawled back to the living room and dialed the memorized number with shaking hands. My voice quivered as I described the situation to the dispatcher.

In a condescending voice, she said, "Why don't you just wait him out, honey. I'm sure he'll go away soon."

My normal self would have responded to anyone with authority with a soft-spoken, "Okay." But from some wellspring of strength, I refused to give in—not this time. "You don't understand. He's sitting there with a rifle aimed at this house. If you don't send someone out here right now, I'll keep calling and calling."

The dispatcher sighed. "Well...okay, I'll see who's in the area."

Five minutes went by. My stomach churned and sweat popped out all over. I was hot and cold at the same time.

Another five minutes passed.

What's taking so long?

I dared peek out the back window, being careful to stay in a shadow. Richard, accustomed to sitting quietly in a deer blind, continued to sit there with the rifle aimed at the house. Fifteen minutes had passed since I called.

Please, dear God, don't let him fire that gun.

I sneaked a more careful look at the gun. I recognized the "thirty aught six" Richard had so often boasted about—along with its powerful scope. I didn't know much about guns, but I knew this one was a potent weapon.

Can it penetrate a house? Can a bullet go through a wall and still wound me?

Twenty minutes had passed. I strained to hear every sound and wished the whoosh-whoosh of blood rushing around my head wasn't so loud.

A car rolled to a stop in front of the house. I made a slit between panels of the curtains that covered the front window. A police officer approached the front door.

At least they didn't come with the sirens screaming.

Remaining half stooped, I opened the front door in time to glimpse a second officer walking cautiously around the side of the house. While I spoke to the first officer, I heard Richard's truck tires crunching in the gravel.

The second officer returned to the front. "He drove away."

The two men looked relieved as they nodded to each other. "Now that he's left," Officer One suggested, "why don't you just go on home and relax? It'll be all right now." I knew from past experience they didn't want to be involved, but I hated the condescension in the officer's voice. The message I heard was, "Be a good little girl, now, and go on home. We big, strong men are taking care of everything."

I had done exactly that in the past, but going away quietly wasn't good enough this time. I demanded to press charges. "But," Officer One explained, "Judge Freeze is probably asleep by now and we'd have to wake him. You don't want to do that, do you?"

"Yes. Yes I do!"

Both officers sighed as though my words were fifty-pound weights settling across their shoulders.

At Judge Freeze's nearby house, my hands shook so badly I was barely able to sign the necessary papers, but I was proud that I had not backed down. *Now* I would agree to go home.

I didn't expect Richard to be arrested, though. The look on the officers' faces plainly said they were merely placating me, and had no intention of pursuing Richard. Still, I took some comfort that I had done all I could.

A couple of minutes later, the officers dropped me back at my house, and I stole into the dark interior, leaving all the lights off. If Richard had followed me to Clarice's, he could have seen me return home. Police cars aren't hard to spot.

Moonlight provided barely enough illumination for me to secure all the doors and windows. That done, I went into the hall in the center of the house and closed all the doors. Cocooned within total darkness, I felt safer somehow. For at least fifteen minutes, I listened hard as I breathed slowly through my mouth. I heard nothing unusual. My heart rate slowed and my breathing quieted.

Why did he do this now? Can't he see that it's just this kind of behavior that drove me to file for divorce, that this is exactly what I want to escape? This time he didn't even use alcohol as an excuse. I'm more determined than ever to get out of this marriage—and soon.

At about ten-thirty, I felt safe enough to reach for the phone. I swiftly opened the door to the bedroom, snatched the phone from just inside the door, uncurled its cord to its full length, and closed the door again. In the pitch black, I felt the numbers to dial Rita.

"The girls are fine," said Rita.

"Have you heard from Richard?" I asked.

"No. What's going on?"

I explained briefly what had happened since the earlier phone call.

"Well, I don't know what's in his mind, but you know the girls are safe here. They want to stay for the night."

"Thanks, Rita. I'll be over to get them in the morning."

They frequently spent the night with my in-laws, and could probably guess that the unexpected change in plans had something do with their dad. They had gone through events like this far too many times. I hoped this would be the last.

Rita was an over-protective mother who routinely defended her son, and I knew she wouldn't approve of what I had done, but I told her anyway so she would be prepared in case he was arrested. This time, even she had little to offer in his defense.

After another hour of sitting in the dark, mulling over my past and future, I felt brave enough to venture into bed. I wasn't brave enough to turn on any lights or change out of my clothes. I closed my eyes hoping for a phone call informing me of Richard's arrest. All that came was fitful sleep and bad dreams.

Chapter 2

Now what?

"Can't I have him ordered to stay away from me, John?" I asked.

At nine o'clock Monday morning I phoned my attorney and described the events of the previous day. Tall and thin, John Tipton was an eager, early-thirties lawyer who had listened with sympathy during our previous meetings. Even though I had told him about some of Richard's past behavior, he reacted to this latest incident with "Really?" and "How scary!"

"Unfortunately, as long as the marriage exists, the law offers you little protection—only prosecution after an offense has taken place. But wait just a minute ..." He paused—a long pause.

I heard papers shuffling. I tried to want patiently, but my foot kept tapping the floor.

Finally, he said, "I'm looking through your file and I think I might be able to help you after all. Give me some time. I'll call you back."

"Please find a way. I don't want to go through another ordeal like that."

An hour and a half later, John called back and said, "I think I have good news, Bettie. I told you before that the divorce hearing couldn't be scheduled until June, but I think I can get it on the docket of the March circuit court, just two weeks from now." His voice seemed more spirited.

"That's great, John."

Two weeks. I think I can make it that long.

"There is a catch, though."

Uh-oh.

"We need to get Richard and his attorney to meet with us this week to work out a final agreement, so the judge merely has to approve it. That's the only way we can get the case on the March docket. Do you think you can get him to do that?"

"Maybe. I'll talk to his mother when I pick up the girls, and see if I can get her on my side. She is the person most likely to persuade him."

When I arrived at the Walkers' an hour later, Karen and Linda were playing in the backyard under the watchful eyes of Richard's parents, Rita and Ed. Linda was making mud pies, which Ed pretended to eat. Karen was dressing her baby doll, and Rita was helping Karen choose outfits.

"Good morning, girls. Looks like you're having fun."

"Where's Daddy?" Five-year-old Karen's expression told me she knew her dad had once again done something bad. After all, he had come to get her and her sister the day before for an afternoon visit. But he didn't return, and they had stayed overnight unexpectedly.

"I don't know, honey." I always hated this part.

What should I say?

I didn't want to turn the girls against their dad, but I also believed I shouldn't lie to them. I usually said as little as necessary.

Linda, three years old, continued to cook, apparently unconcerned.

Karen's questioning look faded into one of resignation. She saw I wasn't going to offer any more information and slowly returned to tugging clothes on her doll.

After a few minutes, I asked Rita if we could go inside and talk. Ed, supplied with a fresh pot of coffee and a full pack of cigarettes, agreed to stay outside with the girls.

Inside with Rita, I explained the possibility of a moved-up court date. "I really need to get this over, so I won't have to be afraid of another day like yesterday. And we both know you're the only one he'll listen to."

"Well, you know I don't approve of this divorce, but you seem determined to go through with it. And after his shenanigans yesterday, I agree with getting it over as soon as possible. I sure wouldn't want him to do anything else to you or to the girls. I'll talk to him."

Shenanigans, indeed! She just admitted how serious it was and yet she still refers to it as though it was harmless teasing.

While she wasn't always on my side, she was very protective of her granddaughters. I knew somewhere deep inside she was afraid he was capable of something worse than "shenanigans."

The following Friday, in the office of his attorney, Richard greeted me cheerfully, as if the last weekend had never happened. "Morning, Bet. You ready to get started."

Today was the charming Richard, the one who emerged after a drinking binge or a fit of temper. He was always sorry for what he had done and willing to promise anything to obtain forgiveness.

I played along with his amnesia to get his cooperation. "Yes, and if we're both reasonable, this shouldn't take long."

After some discussion and suggestions from each attorney, Richard offered to pay child support in the form of the rent and utilities, allowing me to stay in the house. Even though these expenses were less than the child support I had requested, I accepted the offer. I waived alimony altogether and agreed to a clause stating that if I moved out of the house, child support would be one hundred dollars a month. A meager amount, but then I didn't imagine I would move any time soon. On that day, I couldn't afford to think far into the future. I just needed to get the case to court.

With no resistance from Richard, the agreement awarded me full custody of the girls and Richard the right to "reasonable" visitation.

A week later, John Tipton joined my mother and me in an otherwise deserted courtroom in downtown Natchez. Mother had come with me because I was required to provide a witness to

Richard's behavior. At that time in Mississippi there were only two grounds for divorce—adultery or physical abuse. I elected to use the latter.

Richard had the good sense to stay away. His attorney came in, greeted John, and proceeded to the other side of the room.

Soon the judge came in and asked each of us to identify ourselves. He then casually flipped through the final agreement, occasionally interrupting the silence with a question.

Mother and I both described times that Richard drank too much and made threats to me—and one time to her. After hearing the fourth story, the judge nodded and indicated he was satisfied that Richard's behavior was indeed abusive. Without fanfare, he signed the final divorce decree, and quickly disappeared out a side door.

With a rush of relief that it was over so quickly, I floated out of the courthouse feeling a hundred pounds lighter. I thanked John and jokingly told him I hoped I'd never need to see him again. After he walked away, I stood in the warm sun and spring breeze, contemplating my new status.

How fitting for my new beginning to take place in the spring, the time of year for rebirth. Just let Richard threaten me again. Now I have the law to protect me.

But if the future offered safety from Richard, it also held challenges.

Richard didn't support us during the marriage, so why should I expect anything different now?

Even though I now felt reasonably protected from threats from Richard, another burden remained—that of providing for my daughters and myself.

It was that very issue that had spawned my resolve to obtain a bachelor's degree, which I had begun nearly two years earlier. Feeling trapped in a marriage that was growing worse each year, I had descended into despair. It seemed as if I had been at the bottom of a deep, stainless steel well that had no handholds on the sides, and was in danger of drowning.

The only way out of that well appeared to be more education, which I hoped would enable me to earn a decent living for myself and my children.

Even though my financial situation seemed bleak, I was still passionately committed to completing my degree, although I couldn't fathom how. But only a few years earlier it had seemed impossible to even start to college, and now I'd earned almost one third of the hours required for graduation.

Mother interrupted my thoughts. "It's nearly noon. Why don't we have lunch?"

I hadn't realized I was just standing on the sidewalk, frozen in my tracks. "Uh…Oh, that sounds nice. I know a place near here."

We walked to a small, quiet restaurant and selected a corner booth. We both ordered the beverage of the South—iced tea—and made small talk as we looked over the menus.

As Mother squeezed lemon into her tea, her eyebrows pinched and rose. She looked up at me as she poured sugar. "It was worse than I knew, wasn't it?"

When the judge had asked for examples of Richard's abuse, I had described two of the worst incidents—ones she hadn't known about. I hesitated. "Yes…at times it was."

She handed me the sugar.

"I didn't tell you about all of it because you had enough to worry about. Besides, you couldn't have done anything." For a long moment, the only sound was spoons clinking against the sides of iced tea glasses.

Mother sipped, frowned, and looked down. In a low voice, she said, "After hearing about the incidents you described this morning, and thinking back over the ones I already knew about, I'm surprised you stayed with him as long as you did."

"It was complicated. I'm not sure I completely understand why myself." My gaze went out the window and into the past as I remembered the agony of indecision. Glad to be in a relatively secluded location, I tried to explain.

"First, I took my marriage vows seriously—for better or worse, for richer or poorer, in sickness and in health. Then as things got bad, I thought it was partly my fault. If I could just love Richard enough, be a good enough wife, "help" him like he always asked, he'd have to love me back enough to change. As time went by, I gradually realized it wasn't my fault.

"But by then, I felt hopelessly trapped. How could I make it on my own? There were no jobs I was qualified for. Certainly nothing that paid enough to live on. I thought there was no way out, that all I had to look forward to was a miserable, hopeless future."

She took a Kleenex from her purse and wiped at her eyes. "I wish I had been more help to you. I guess I didn't want to admit how disastrous the situation was. I didn't want to think about my daughter living in such circumstances and enduring such treatment. Besides, since you knew I thought you were too young to get married in the first place, I was afraid anything I might say would sound like 'I told you so.' Not a very good excuse, I'm afraid." We both looked up and our eyes met. Regret pooled and shimmered on her lower eyelids. She dabbed again.

I looked away and quickly took a sip of cold tea and held it in my mouth, hoping to stanch the threatening flow in my own eyes. "It's okay, Mom. I understand. Beside, Daddy discussed it with me."

"I thought maybe he had. Since he had been through a divorce himself, I figured he understood a lot better than I did."

"Yeah, I guess he did. Not long before he passed away, he told me about his divorce. After one of my bad weekends, Daddy must have seen my struggle to make a decision. Standing at the kitchen sink washing his coffee pot, he said, 'Bet, I know you take your marriage vows seriously. And you should. But one person simply can't make a marriage. It takes both.'

"'Now, when I got married to my first wife, I thought I loved her as much as anybody could. We had three children together and I thought everything was fine. But then a couple of my friends told me she was running around on me, and then I found out she was making charges all over town behind my back. I tried to ignore it but, well…after a while, she killed all the love I ever had for her. And the way I figured it, when there's no love left, there's no marriage. That's when I decided to divorce her, and I've never regretted it.'

"Then he looked straight at me and said, 'Now, Bet, I'm not telling you what to do, but I believe when a marriage is dead, when all the love has been killed, then maybe divorce isn't wrong.'"

Mother smiled slightly. "That's interesting. You know, he never said much to me about his first wife, about why he divorced her, and I never probed. About all he talked about was his concern about remarrying after being divorced. You know how devoutly he tried to follow Biblical teachings. He said he prayed long and hard about it, and came to believe that God could not possibly be against his loving someone as much as he loved me."

Speaking of Daddy brought irrepressible smiles to both of us. Vivid images sprang to mind, and I remembered how much he had loved Mother. He cherished her until the day he died, flirting with her in his playful, boyish way. The familiar image of him walking up behind her and kissing her on the neck played out on the windowpanes. The look on Mother's face told me she was reflecting on her own fond memories.

The server brought our food, interrupting our reverie.

"Then why *did* it take you so long to decide to get a divorce?"

Daddy had been gone a year and a half, having passed away in November 1967.

I took a deep breath and exhaled slowly. "I'm not sure." I looked out the window at a cloud drifting by. "See that cloud out there? It isn't in control of its path. It only goes where the wind blows it. I think I was like that. I exerted little will of my own, but simply reacted to the people around me—especially Richard *and* his mother."

Mother didn't say anything, but nodded slightly.

"I didn't realize that for a long time." I picked at a cuticle. "It goes beyond that, though. I don't think I truly understand why I married Richard in the first place. Looking back now, it seems such an obviously foolish, immature decision. And I don't really know why I stayed with him for so long."

"It might take some time, Bettie, but it'll make sense one day."

I thought back to when I met Richard.

Why was I so attracted to him? Why didn't I see the early warning signs? Why hadn't I listened to the small voice in my head? Why had I been so determined to make the marriage work?

Contemplating the past, I said, "I was such a wallflower…"

Chapter 3

Will He Ask Me Out?

April 1960

"You wanna dance?"
Did he really ask me to dance?

Something more than his long legs, lean body, sandy-brown hair, and sky-blue eyes had drawn my attention when he walked in. Maybe it was the way he stood with his weight on one leg and his hip sticking out to the side or the slightly one-sided smile or the way he tilted his head—or what passed for self-assurance.

We were at a party on Lake St. John, just outside my tiny hometown of Ferriday, Louisiana. Natchez, Mississippi was only twelve miles away, on the other side of the Mississippi River. Compared to my small town, Natchez seemed like a big city.

I never knew who invited Richard and his Natchez friends to the party, but their arrival unquestionably changed the mood. Before they got there, we were just a group of friends having fun. After they walked in, someone lowered the lights and put on slower, softer music. The girls, with a subconscious effort, engaged in the age-old ritual of attracting the attention of the boys.

Soon after Richard came in, our eyes met briefly as he flashed what I thought might be a flirty beam at me.

I'm sure he looks at all the girls like that. It doesn't mean a thing.

I focused on the chips and dip, trying not to pay attention to him. I almost spilled my soda when he appeared by my side saying,

"Hi. My name's Richard. What's yours?" From up close, his eyes seemed even brighter blue.

"Bettie." My heart thumped so loudly I was afraid he could hear it. My face grew strangely warm.

"So, this is a prom-protest party, huh?" he said with a sideways grin.

"Yeah, sort of. Some of us who, uh…didn't get invited to the prom, well…we decided to have our own party." I swallowed hard and cleared my throat, which felt oddly constricted.

"Looks like everybody's having a good time." He looked out over the large room. "What about you?"

"Yeah, I'm having fun."

He looked back at me. "No, I mean, tell me something about you."

"Oh, I'm…uh…I live outside Ferriday. On a farm."

Why did I say that? He'll probably think I'm a farm hick.

"A farm girl, huh?" He smiled and winked.

Okay, so maybe that wasn't such a bad thing to say.

"Uh…sort of. Actually, my dad raises cattle."

"Oh, so he's really a rancher. Tell me more."

I couldn't get enough air. I couldn't think.

Calm down. Think of something to tell him.

"I play the piano and also play flute in the band."

What else can I say? Should I tell him the truth—that I'm boring, that I've never been on a date?

But then Richard asked me to dance—to a slow song. My heart raced even faster and my skin tingled when he reached for my hand, but then dancing seemed easier than talking at the moment. Our mismatched heights—six two and five two—gave me the sense of being enveloped. His shoulders were just the right height for my head to lean into, his long arms draped around me. His chin rested lightly on the top of my head. All of which made me acutely aware of my femaleness. Little did I know those moments were giving birth to an attraction that would prove to be ill-fated.

I wasn't pretty, nor did I possess the charm that comes so naturally to popular girls. Truth be told, I was homely and awkward. Or at least that's what I believed. Before that night, I had no reason to believe otherwise. In ninth and tenth grades, my friend Susan and I had gone to school dances and watched the boys walk past us as if we were invisible. We simply weren't the kind of girls boys noticed—at least not in the way we wanted to be noticed.

Best friends since third grade, Susan and I returned to the dances, each time wishing and dreaming for a better outcome. No surprise we were at the party for those *not* invited to the prom.

The party was at a friend's lake house, with the usual food, records, games, parents—and boys, but only those who were our pals. The girls were to sleep over, and the boys were invited to return the next morning to swim. We had been dancing—mostly girls with girls. Until the Natchez boys arrived. Then everything changed.

By asking me to dance, Richard had rescued me from being "everybody's friend, no one's girlfriend," if only momentarily. Richard's smile reminded me of country music singer Jimmy Dean, and he looked at me in a way I hadn't experienced before. I recognized the look, though. I had seen it on the faces of other boys looking at other girls. I could hardly believe someone now looked at me with that special smile—one that said I like you.

Before the boys left for the night, Richard and I danced several more times and he promised to return the next day. After he left, the girls peppered me with questions. "What did you talk about?" "How old is he?" "Where does he live?" "Did he ask you for your phone number?" Giddy from Richard's attention, I blushed and giggled.

Later, while everyone else slept, I lay in my sleeping bag preparing myself for disappointment.

He won't be back. He's not actually interested in me. Who would be?

I finally drifted off to sleep, almost convinced he wouldn't return, but with hope lurking in the back of my mind.

The next morning, I walked with a group of girls—all of us in our swimsuits and carrying towels—toward the lake for a swim. I noticed the back of someone launching a boat. When he turned around, I saw that it was Richard. He *had* come back after all. At the sight of him, my heart did flip-flops.

Is he still interested?

When he spotted me walking toward him, he answered my question with a smile that lit up his face. He paused, and with a piercing gaze, he winked and whistled. "Hey there, pretty legs. Where'ya headed?" I didn't think I had a single feature a boy would find attractive, and yet he had found something to compliment.

Trying to sound casual, I answered, "We're going for a swim."

He raised one eyebrow. "Wanna come with me in the boat instead?"

"This is your boat?"

"Yeah." He swelled with pride.

"How old are you anyway?" I didn't know any high school students who owned a boat.

"I'm nineteen. Didn't I tell you last night?"

Nineteen!

A four-year age difference was huge. "No, you didn't. I didn't realize you're out of school."

"That make a difference?"

"No...I guess not."

What would my parents say about me dating a nineteen year old? But I don't have anything to be concerned about yet. For all I know, I might never see him after today.

After he situated his car and the boat trailer, he helped me into the ski boat. A few others came with us, but Richard invited me to sit beside him. I didn't think I'd ever been so flattered. I'd never been in the "girlfriend" role before. Also, I'd never ridden in a fast boat. It was exhilarating in more ways than one. We swept almost the full length of the long lake with Richard showing off the boat's speed and making sweeping turns. And my heart was swept away by Richard's attention.

For the next few hours, Richard simultaneously flirted with me and towed skiers, maneuvering the boat with considerable flamboyance all the while. I struggled to return his flirtations with at least a little poise and wit, but I was clearly a novice. Even so, by afternoon's end Richard had asked me for my phone number and promised to call. By then, my heart was hopelessly swept up in its own swift-flowing current, unable to reverse direction.

I virtually levitated as a friend drove me home. Bubbling with excitement, I could hardly wait to spill out the news to my parents.

"Guess what? I met a boy last night who asked me to dance. He took me on his boat today and asked me for my phone number."

Daddy, ever the optimist, smiled with a twinkle in his eye, clearly pleased to see me so happy. It had been almost as painful for him as for me when I had come home from dances week after week, and he had asked, "Bet, did you dance?"

Time after time, I had answered, "No, not tonight."

And time after time, Daddy reassured me. "You will, Bet, you will."

Mother's face registered more concern than joy, but any other reaction from her would have been shocking. She worried first and asked questions later. Also, she would have been happy for me to postpone any interest in boys for a few more years.

Hardworking and independent, my parents were defined by strong religious beliefs and practices. "Propriety" governed every aspect of my mother's life, including the way she dressed—modest and plain. A registered nurse, she was of average height and just slightly plump. She kept her brown hair short and neat, her only makeup modest amounts of powder and lipstick. She considered my attempts to be just the teeniest bit glamorous to be cheap and tawdry.

Daddy, a cattle rancher, was much older than Mother—a remarkable twenty-nine years to be exact. Even though his moral code ran as deeply as Mother's, his main concerns were far different from hers. Following rules was less important to him than intentions. And he was much less concerned about the opinions of others than she. Perhaps his self-assuredness had come with age. Whereas Mother put great store in appearances—*What will people think?* still echoes in my brain—Daddy followed his own internal voice.

Small and wiry, he stood no taller than five foot seven in his prime, his only hair a dark blonde/gray fringe around the sides of his head. He boasted that he weighed a hundred thirty-five pounds at his heaviest, in spite of his lifelong attempt to gain weight. Every pound must have been muscle, though, because he pulled his weight when working alongside men twice his size.

Mother, in her effort to instill modesty in me, overreached her goal. Rather than merely preventing me from being conceited, her constant admonishments and criticisms wore away my confidence. Little that I did met her exacting standards. She routinely pointed out every mistake or omission down to the tiniest detail.

When I was about ten, Mother made it perfectly plain to me that I was perfectly plain. I had performed recently in a piano recital, and the group photo had just arrived in the mail. As she and I sat looking at the photograph, she commented that one of the other girls was "right pretty." Now she never told me the difference between "pretty" and "right pretty," but her tone led me to believe she meant "*almost* pretty, but not quite." Never once did I hear her pronounce anyone an outright pretty.

That day, yearning to believe I was attractive, I asked her if she thought I was pretty. She looked away, then back at the photograph, and finally said, "Well..., you know every mama crow thinks her baby is the blackest." Her hesitation, followed by the adage, sent me an unmistakable message, *No, I don't, but because I'm your mother, I'm obligated to say you are.* I had heard her use that phrase before and it was always meant to say that all parents are biased toward their own, even if the opinion is not shared by others. The fact that she didn't think I was pretty burned itself deeper into my brain each time I stood at my dresser, looked into the mirror, and saw a plain face looking back.

Daddy's gentle, loving voice of approval stood in stark contrast, but was hard to hear over Mother's harsher, insistent tones. His subtle messages weren't recognized or appreciated until many years later.

~~~~~

On that Saturday, after telling my parents about meeting Richard, even Mother couldn't repress a small smile when she saw the joy on my face. However, when they asked how old he was, and I answered "nineteen," her smile faded and she looked at my dad with a concerned look. He just winked at me.

"We know you're excited, honey, but go slow and be careful," Mother said.

At fifteen, and in the throes of first love, I didn't know how to go slow, and couldn't comprehend how to be careful. Not when I was on the brink of having a dream fulfilled.

Chapter 4

But He Does Care

"**R**ing, ring."

The sound sliced through the Sunday afternoon quiet. For as long as I could remember, Sunday afternoons found my parents in their room with the newspaper and heavy eyelids. My brother and I had long ago been trained to maintain quiet until we heard our parents up and about.

Our phone resided on an old-fashioned phone bench—a seat with an attached arm, similar to old school desks. It occupied a nook in the end of the hall between the kitchen and living room, at the opposite end of the hall from the bedrooms. In our small house, though, no place was very far away from any other.

Racing to reach the phone, I banged my knee into the door frame. I stopped to take a breath before picking up, crossed my fingers, and prayed it was Richard.

"Hello?"

"Hey, Bettie, it's Richard. Whatcha' doin'?"

My throat constricted. I couldn't breathe. Silently I shouted, *It's him—he really called!* I struggled to find my voice again.

"Reading the paper." I didn't dare tell him the truth—that I had been anxiously pacing in my room, hoping for the phone to ring. I curled up on the seat, put my feet up on the arm, and began twisting the phone cord with my free hand. "What're you doing?"

"Calling you, silly."

I was acutely aware my parents could hear my end of the conversation, which exacerbated my nervousness. Later on, I perfected the technique of slipping the short phone cord under the door to the living room, and sitting on the floor next to the closed door to have slightly more privacy. But I hadn't yet figure out that move. That afternoon I was self-conscious, knowing my parents were listening attentively to every word.

After reminiscing about the party, Richard asked, "Hey, you want to go to a movie Friday night?"

"Yes" fell out of my mouth before I could blink.

As I untangled the phone cord and replaced the receiver, I almost floated, as if filled with helium. To keep the imperative Sunday quiet, I squelched shouts of glee. Instead, I padded through the kitchen and out onto the back porch before squealing under my breath, *He really called. He asked me out. I have a date—a real date!*

After the reality of it settled in, delight gave way to anxiety. Would my parents agree? And how could I wait five days? My eagerness reminded me of my excitement when I was four and five waiting for Christmas, when each day dragged by and a week was an eternity.

~~~~~~~

"Who was that on the phone earlier this afternoon?" Mother bit her lip as her eyebrows almost came together.

"It was Richard. The boy I told you about? The one I met at the party. He asked me out on Friday night."

"Where does he want to take you?"

"Just to a movie."

Please say it's okay. I'll die if you say no.

"Well, okay, but you'd better be home early."

"I will."

Thank goodness.

Mother nearly stifled her smile; she couldn't manage to completely quash her amusement at seeing me so excited.

The days crawled by, and Friday finally arrived, bringing both exhilaration and nervousness. I agonized over what to wear, and took twice the usual amount of time getting dressed. Satisfied I had done the best I could, and just before the appointed time of seven o'clock, I began to pace back and forth in front of the kitchen window.

Our house sat on a gravel road just a bit more than a half-mile south of Highway 84 that sliced through Ferriday and Natchez. The wide window over the kitchen sink faced north toward the highway. At night, from that window, we could follow the car lights and tell if a car on the highway slowed and turned. If slowing headlights vanished, we knew the car had turned away from us, but if they appeared, we knew the car had turned in our direction. The kitchen window became my spot for waiting, watching—and worrying.

No worrying this night, though. Right on time, I saw a car coming from the east slow as it approached our turn. Then its headlights appeared. The lights blinked through the trees that lined the gravel road as the car traveled nearer. My breathing grew shallow and the knots in my stomach tightened when I heard to gravel in our driveway crunch. I hovered near the back door, waiting for the knock.

The knock came from the front door, though. Richard couldn't yet know that we rarely used the front door. I darted from the back of the house to the front. Richard stood with his weight on one leg, just as I remembered him from the party. Grinning, he looked even more handsome than I remembered, in a blue pinpoint oxford shirt and khaki slacks. I offered him a seat and went to get my parents.

Most evenings found Mother in the kitchen wearing an old smock, and Daddy in the living room watching TV in worn jeans. Tonight, though, Mother had on a nice dress and Daddy had changed into slacks and a dress shirt.

They had no experience meeting their teenage daughter's date. I didn't know what to expect, and was grateful Daddy didn't grill Richard. Mother spent more effort performing a visual critique than speaking. After a brief exchange of pleasantries, Richard led me to his car.

In an unpracticed sort of way, he opened the door of his '59 red and white Chevy, helped me in, and gently closed the door. Such attention from an "older man" caused a subtle transformation to begin. In those few moments, a girl began to slip away, and a woman began to appear. Or so I imagined.

I don't remember the name of the movie—I was too distracted—but we saw it at the Grande, the nicest theater in Natchez. After the movie, Richard took me to the Monmouth Drive-in, one of the two main hangouts for teenagers in Natchez. Over burgers and shakes, we began finding out about each other.

He learned church was a vital part of my life; I learned he rarely attended. I learned his family was in the oil business; he learned my mother was a nurse and my dad a cattle rancher. I knew as little about the oil industry as he did about cattle ranching or nursing. He learned I was sheltered and innocent; he presented himself as quite experienced. Our differences served not to put distance between us, but to make the other more intriguing.

He monitored his watch to ensure he returned me home on time. There, he walked me to the door and said goodnight with a tender kiss on the cheek. It was not the kiss of a shy, unsure boy, but the deliberately restrained kiss of a man, or so I thought. As he walked away, he looked back over his shoulder and said, "I'll call you soon."

I hoped he had enjoyed the evening as much as I had. Impressed that he had not only been fun to be with, but also that he showed such respect saying goodnight, I wanted to believe he was serious when he said he'd call soon, but I still prepared for disappointment.

Apparently he was serious, though, because soon turned out to be the next day. We made a date for the following Friday; this time phone calls during the week eased the anxiety of waiting. Before I knew it, I had developed the habit of springing to the phone each time it rang.

Patterns take hold quickly, so the third Friday night date came as no surprise. That evening, as usual, I stood at the kitchen window watching for car lights. Five after seven and no turning car.

What could have happened? I hope nothing's wrong. I hope he didn't have an accident.

Fifteen minutes late, then twenty. By seven thirty, I concluded he wasn't coming, but I was more worried than angry. I was confident something had happened beyond this control.

Richard phoned the next day to apologize, explaining he had worked late and "there ain't no telephones hangin' off those trees, ya know," a phrase I would hear too often, and grow to detest. At the time, though, it sounded perfectly reasonable, since he worked at remote oil well sites in the countryside. I accepted his apology.

Susan was dating her first boyfriend, too, so we compared notes later that day. Her boyfriend had stood her up before, too, and so we thought this must be normal.

Jo Ann, Marie, and Mary Beth were not dating, but were eager to listen to Susan's and my reports, vicariously enjoying our emerging relationships. In Monday's homeroom, they were less tolerant than Susan—maybe because they were simply disappointed I had nothing to report except a phone call and an apology. Their question-mark eyebrows signaled they wouldn't have been so quick to accept Richard's explanation.

A few Fridays later, I again watched from the kitchen window, only to be disappointed by Richard's failure to appear. This time he called later the same evening, and explained he had car trouble, but his voice sounded different. He laughed more than usual and seemed distracted. I heard loud voices in the background. I wondered why the problem with his car had prevented him from calling earlier, but I dismissed the concern just as easily as I ignored the eye rolls on Monday when I told Marie and Mary Beth about the car-trouble explanation. Even Susan doubted his excuse that time.

A week later, Richard arrived promptly for our customary Friday night date. Wearing a confident smile, he ignored the subject of the broken date. If I clung to any doubts about his sincerity, they were soon erased. Before we reached the highway, he stopped the car on the side of the road.

"Why are we stopping here?" I asked. "Is something wrong?"

"No, nothing's wrong. In fact, I think something's right. Bettie, do you know how much I like you? I hope you like me, too, because I want us to go steady. Will you wear my class ring?"

"Yes," I answered with no hesitation.

Yes, of course I'll wear your ring. I'm yours, all yours.

He removed the ring from his finger and put it on mine. Flattery earned, among other things, complete forgiveness, and what was more flattering than being asked to go steady? I forgot he'd ever failed to show up as planned. One class ring wiped the slate clean.

~~~~~~

The next day I couldn't suppress a giddy smile as I showed off the ring. Multiple layers of adhesive tape kept it on—left hand, ring finger, of course. Susan, Mary Beth, Jo Ann, and Marie all beamed, too, as if the ring partially belonged to them. Susan had just broken up with her boyfriend, so all of them saw the ring as a symbol of hope. In little more than two months, I had gone from dateless to going steady. If it happened to me, it could happen to them, too, couldn't it?

Richard had added a Saturday night date and sometime a Sunday afternoon drive to the usual weekend routine. The Sunday afternoon drives included places such as the many antebellum homes in Natchez, the Natchez Trace, and the rural countryside with its plentiful oil wells. Sometimes we spent part of the afternoon with his parents, who had warmly welcomed me into their family.

Weeks turned into months. My parents had cautioned me to take it slow, but their advice wasn't audible over the roar of that fast-flowing current, the one in which I continued to be swept along by Richard's charm, flattery, and, most importantly, his professed fondness of me.

Each date night began with watching traffic from the kitchen window. Richard's initial punctuality had given way to tardiness, so I didn't usually give up my post for at least an hour. Only then would I sheepishly retreat to my room, hoping to complete my getaway with no comments from my parents.

Sometimes Richard called the same evening to explain, sometimes I didn't hear from him until the next day. But he always had a great excuse! Most of the time he said had to work late, and then repeated "...and there aren't any telephones hanging off those trees, ya know."

~~~~~

"Bettie, how can you put up with someone so inconsiderate? Is this the kind of person you want to date?" Mother had intercepted my retreat one evening in early September.

"He's not inconsiderate. He doesn't miss dates on purpose. It's just that sometimes he has to work late. And, like he says, there are no telephones on the trees out in the oilfield."

"Well, I just don't like seeing you disappointed so often. If he really cared about you, he wouldn't treat you this way."

"But he does care, Mom." In truth, it did hurt each time he stood me up, but I couldn't admit it to anyone, especially to myself. A small, persistent voice in my head—my own better judgment, or maybe an angel—warned me about Richard's unreliability, about getting my heart broken. I cleverly ignored that voice.

In the center of my being, I needed Richard to want me. Rejecting this boy who said he liked me, who had asked me to go steady, who had said I had pretty legs, was unthinkable.

Chapter 5

He Must be the One

October 1960

"Richard, stop." Richard's hand had deftly unfastened a couple of buttons on my blouse and now edged inside my bra.

"Oh, come on, Bet. Why not?"

"Because. I've told you before, I don't want us to get carried away and end up going all the way."

For a couple of months now our dates had included parking and making out. And for nearly that long Richard had challenged what I considered permissible limits. The burden had become all mine to prevent us from crossing the forbidden line.

My parents, along with years of Sunday School and Church every week, had produced in me a strong, vigilant conscience. As much as I wanted Richard to want me, I also wanted to remain a "good girl." In spite of my efforts, though, Richard had cajoled me into moving the line in increments ever so slight. We had even gotten dangerously close to abandoning all restraint a few times, but I had pulled us back from the brink just in time.

On this typical Friday night, we had started out at the Sandwich Bar, an octagonal-shaped drive-in, Ferriday's only gathering place for teenagers. We had milk shakes and oyster burgers—a Sandwich Bar specialty—while we visited with our friends. Now we had relocated to our customary non-public parking spot.

The gravel road that ran south from the highway to our house continued on for another mile to the southwest corner of our property, then turned east and continued for another half mile or so. The last half mile had no houses and wide shoulders, which made it a convenient place for parking. My parents were unaware of this circumstance, and I wasn't about to tell them.

On the red bench seat of the '59 Chevy, with the Everly Brothers' "Wake up, Little Susie" streaming from the radio, Richard lifted my chin with one hand and looked into my eyes. "Bettie, don't you see how much I care for you? I don't just love you, but I'm in love with you. Don't you love me too?"

"Are you sure? Do you mean it?" This was the first time he had ever declared he was in love with me. Everyone knew that *in love with* was on a whole different level than a simple *I love you.*

He drew me closer as the Everly Brothers gave way to the Drifters singing "Save the Last Dance for Me."

"Yes, of course I mean it, Bet. And you love me, too. I know you do." A long kiss followed, tongues exploring and probing, the hand once again worming its way into my bra, this time with newfound courage, unchallenged. The declaration of love had apparently fueled his passion and determination.

The words had a decidedly different effect on me. They befuddled my brain, leaving me unable to think. The hand relocated from my blouse to my thigh, slipped effortlessly under my skirt, and inched upward.

My heart rate increased, not in response to his actions, but to those powerful words echoing in my head. *"I'm in love with you."* I almost forgot to pay attention to what he was doing, but suddenly realized he was approaching the most recent limit. My hand stopped his.

He broke the kiss and pleaded, "You know we're in love and we're gonna get married, so what's the difference if we wait or not? If you really loved me, you'd want this as much as I do." He removed my hand from his and placed it over the bulge in his pants.

He had just increased the stakes once again. He had casually mentioned the possibility of getting married, but now he spoke as if it was decided—a certainty.

The battle in my head raged.

I know this is wrong, and what if I get pregnant? I'd be humiliated. But he says he loves me, that we're going to get married. I want show him that I really love him. I couldn't stand it if he broke up with me.

His hand slithered ever closer to its target. My hand remained where he had placed it, but it didn't perform as he wanted. The argument not yet settled, I hesitated to remove it. The little voice of warning in my head tried to get my attention. I ignored it.

"Are you really serious about getting married?" I asked.

"Of course. Aren't you?"

"I don't know. I guess."

"I've never been more serious about anything in my life. Don't you see? I'm in love with you, Bettie." His voice was barely above a whisper. His blue eyes radiated a warmth that spread through me and drew me to him.

Expectation of marriage elevated our relationship to a spiritual level, and intoxicated me with love, or, in truth, with *being loved.* I was unable to resist his wishes. "I'm in love with you, too, Richard." I pressed my hand against his hardness and leaned into him, indicating my willingness. Buttons were unbuttoned, zippers unzipped, and clothing rearranged, all with no protest.

~~~~~~~~

Afterward, Richard slowly moved away, smiling and sighing. No trace of regret showed on his face—only satisfaction. His eyebrows rose into a question mark when he saw no such smile on my face. "Are you all right?"

"Yeah, sure." At that moment, however, I really didn't know how I was. Emotions floated just out of reach, not yet taking form.

"You don't look very happy." He was right. I wasn't happy. He tilted his head to one side, and the corners of his mouth turned down, intended to mimic a sad clown. Neither his attempt at a comical face, nor the Coasters' humorous "Charlie Brown" coming from the radio, made me smile.

As I replaced and arranged my clothes, which I had a sudden urgency to do, the unidentified emotions acquired the shape of shame and guilt. I breathed deeply to stop tears that I didn't want Richard to see.

As we finished getting ourselves back together, I wondered if Richard's satisfaction was only physical, or from the fact that he had finally overcome my resistance, or maybe because he thought it meant I really loved him, too. Or maybe it was a combination of all three.

As far as my own fleshly pleasure, there hadn't been much. Years later I came to understand that my only real yearning had been the desire for romance and the need to be wanted. I desperately wanted to earn Richard's love. At that moment, though, I was aware of nothing except my burgeoning guilt.

Richard watched me closely. A dark cloud surrounded us.

"Please take me home now."

Richard looked disappointed, but he put the car in gear and began to drive.

"What's wrong, Bet? Didn't you like it?"

"I don't want to talk about it. Just take me home."

We remained silent for the few minutes it took to complete our normal ruse. So that we didn't approach my house from the wrong direction, we drove from the parking spot at the end of the road back past my house and all the way back to the highway, turned around, waited about five minutes, and then returned to my house. By the time we reached my driveway that night, the silence was leaden. Goodbyes were brief.

I entered the house quietly, relieved to find my parents in their room and—I hoped—asleep. After gathering a fresh nightgown, I padded softly to the bathroom, turned on the water, and poured in a generous amount of bubble bath. Undressing quickly, I dropped each article of clothing into the dirty clothes hamper as if it were contaminated. Indeed, I felt contaminated, too. The little voice was back, insistent on being heard, chastising me.

Why did I let him have his way?

Slipping into the warm, soapy water, I thought about what I regretted the most. I decided there were primarily two things. First, it had not occurred on my wedding night. Second, it wasn't the glorious, romantic experience I had dreamed about. The more I thought about it, the more my guilt mushroomed, until I was filled to the brim with shame and anguish.

I soaked and scrubbed and sobbed. I needed to wash away my misdeed. I needed to cleanse my soul along with my body. When the weeping at last subsided, I rinsed with clean, clear water, still trying to expunge the guilt and wash my sin down the drain.

As I stepped out of the tub and pulled a towel around me, I vowed never to give in to Richard again. By never allowing it to happen again, I could regain my virginity, at least in my heart. Thus, I could reclaim my good girl status.

In my room, I slipped under the covers, and in the darkness pleaded to God for forgiveness, promising not to repeat the transgression and asking for the strength to keep the promise.

I drifted off to sleep rehearsing my defense argument.

It's wrong, Richard. What if I get pregnant? What if someone catches us? We must wait until we're married.

On our next few dates, I kept my vow, even in the face of Richard's most persuasive pleas. But then, Richard brought yet one more arrow from his quiver. He announced his plan to give me an engagement ring for Christmas—an outward, official symbol of our love and commitment. How could I refuse him after that? I yielded again. This time the shame wasn't as sharp as the first time. A week later, my feeble protests were powerless, since I had so recently given in.

In time, the guilt faded, and I came to believe that if I wanted to keep my man's affection, I must give in to his desire for sex. I hushed the little voice, refusing to hear it for quite some time to come.

Concern about the risk of pregnancy didn't fade, though. Curing my ignorance about contraception proved to be difficult. I had already learned that much of the information from my friends was incorrect. *Ladies' Home Journal* and *Reader's Digest* had provided most of my knowledge about sex and pregnancy. But neither magazines nor friends provided enough specific information. Richard used a condom most of the time, but sometimes he convinced me it wasn't necessary because he had determined I was in a "safe" interval.

I prayed a lot.

My parents didn't allow the engagement ring for Christmas, insisting I was too young for such a serious commitment at sixteen. No matter. Ring or no ring, formally engaged or not, our now-regular physical intimacy signified a pledge just as solemn as a formal one, a sort of private betrothal.

Not that anyone else would have wanted me, but I believed our physical union now bound us to each other for eternity. Surely, being loved was so rare and mystical that it seldom happened more than once in a lifetime. I was blessed it had happened at all. Clearly, Richard was my one and only love. If I gave him up, I would be doomed to live out the rest of my life in utter loneliness.

It was no longer a question of *if* I wanted him for my mate. I was now his for life.

Chapter 6

Why Wait?

March 1961

"I'll probably go to LSU. It's not so far away, and I want to stay close to home. What about you two?" Jo Ann shuffled several college brochures on the table in fifth period study hall. She and Marie had finished their homework; I was still working on mine.

Marie picked up a brochure. "I'm going to Northwestern. When we went there for band competition, I liked the campus, and I hear the math department is good."

I looked up to see their expectant faces, as they waited to hear my selection. "I haven't thought about it."

Jo Ann's head jerked up. "Why not?"

"For one thing, I don't know what I'd major in. Music is what I love, but I don't have the talent. My brother's got that. Besides, with Carter in college, I don't think my parents can afford to send me, too."

"Have they said that?" Marie looked puzzled.

"No, but I hear them talking. It's a struggle for them to come up with Carter's tuition. And he'll still have one more year to go after I graduate. I just don't think they can afford two of us in school at the same time."

"If you don't go to college, what will you do?"

"I'll probably get married. Richard keeps saying we're going to as soon as I'm out of school."

Only a few years earlier, I dreamed of becoming a doctor, or a missionary, or both, so that I could do brave and noble work in some exotic part of the world. I would save hundreds of sick children, or perhaps even entire villages. The dream included whatever college would be required for any such work, although the exact nature of such requirement seemed vague at the time.

But those aspirations had faded soon after I began dating Richard, and had now disappeared entirely. My only ambition now was pleasing Richard.

My parents felt duty-bound to send their son to college if he wanted to go, and he had. He wanted to become an electrical engineer. Although I never heard them say so, I sensed they didn't feel the same obligation to their daughter. I wasn't resentful, because I had great passion for a career, and therefore no strong desire to go to college. Like many girls in the fifties and sixties, I expected nothing more from life than to get married and raise kids.

I was more than willing to be swept along by Richard's plans for us to get married.

~~~~~~

"You know, there's no reason we have to wait another year to get married," Richard said. "Why not just do it this year?"

On a clear, warm Saturday night, the first weekend in April, we sipped the shakes we had brought with us from the Sandwich Bar and enjoyed the full moon and plentiful stars in our usual parking spot.

"That sounds good, but I'm sure my parents wouldn't let me get married this year." But the idea had a certain appeal. Being married would give me adult status, which I was eager to have. Besides, Richard wanted me *now*. What if he got tired of waiting?

Richard bolstered his argument. "With my new job, I can easily support us. Why wait?"

"My parents are worried about more than money," I countered. "There's no way they'll give me permission to get married this year. I'm only sixteen. Besides, they'd be afraid people would think we have to get married. They would be mortally embarrassed."

The moonlight accentuated the furrow in his brow as Richard pondered the idea. "Well... don't ask them. Tell them. And if they don't agree, we'll find another way."

"Why don't we just wait until after I graduate?"

"Because I want to be with you every day, and all night." He drew me closer. "Don't you want to be able to stay together all the time? And have our own place? I'm tired of living with my parents. I'm a man now and I want my own place. I want spend all night with you, snuggling. I want to wake up in the morning with you. I'm tired of having to take you home and then go home to my parents' house."

It didn't occur to me until years later that he didn't have the courage to simply move out and live alone. His parents would have made every effort to block him, and he wouldn't have been able to overcome their resistance. If I viewed getting married as my admission ticket into adulthood, Richard must have viewed it as his escape from parental control.

At the moment, though, none of those thoughts crossed my mind—only his flattering words that penetrated a vulnerable spot in my heart. Not for the first time, images of us living together played out in my imagination. I pictured us together in our own place. I would spend my days decorating, cleaning, and cooking, creating a loving home. Richard would spend his days working hard to support us. I'd have a delicious dinner on the table every night. There would be lots of hugs and kisses and romantic weekends. Perhaps the most important would be no parents telling us what to do.

The scene was idyllic, of course, with overwhelming emotional appeal to the girl-wanting-to-be-a-woman.

I didn't like the idea of running away to get married, which would have been the only way without my parents' permission. As backward as Louisiana might have been, a person under eighteen couldn't get married without a parent's consent. Underage couples in our area routinely went to nearby Arkansas to get married, where it was apparently easier. We knew about several who had made the trip; all of them *had* to get married. Eloping to Arkansas carried a stigma I didn't care to have attached to us. After considering the options, I agreed to try to persuade my parents to grant us their permission.

Richard and I planned and dreamed and schemed for another hour, until we realized with a start that my midnight curfew had passed. We hurriedly executed the drive-out-and-back-in-again tactic to get me home as quickly as possible.

At nearly twelve-thirty, I hoped my stealthiest tiptoeing would get me to my room undetected. As I neared my parents' bedroom door, adjacent to mine, Mother's sleepy voice said, "You're home late."

Why does she have to be awake?

"I know. I'm sorry," I whispered through the slight crack in the door. "Richard and I were talking and we lost track of time."

"Talking about what? Nothing's wrong, I hope." Her voice instantly shifted from drowsy to wide-awake. I could imagine her head lifting off the pillow.

"No, nothing's wrong."

Just go ahead and fuss at me for being late and then let me go on to bed.

"Well, it must have been something mighty important to keep you out so late." Her voice had turned sarcastic.

She's not going to drop it. I might as well get it out.

"Uh… Well, we decided we want to get married this June, instead of waiting until next year." I thought I heard her heart pounding, and maybe I could have if my own hadn't been thumping so loudly in my ears.

"What brought this on?" I could imagine her knitted eyebrows and pressed lips. I knew what she was wondering.

"I'm not pregnant, if that's what you're thinking."

At least I don't think I am.

I had no reason to suspect I was pregnant, but an ever-present fear lurked in the back of my mind. "We just want to go ahead and get married this year. We know we're going to get married anyway, so what's the difference if we wait another year or not?"

More silence. "Well...you go on to bed for now. We'll talk about it tomorrow."

I knew Mother wanted to talk to Daddy before any further discussion with me. I also knew I would hear endlessly about how I had caused her to lie awake for hours.

In my hometown in 1961, out-of-wedlock pregnancy brought shame to both the couple and their families. During the next few days, I heard enough snippets of exchanges between my parents to know what they were thinking. Their greatest fear was that if they resisted the marriage, I would end up pregnant. My mother wasn't brave enough to come right out and ask me if we were having sex, because she didn't want to know if the answer was yes. And I tried to give the impression we weren't, of course. But they knew that even if we weren't already sexually active, we likely would be before another year had passed. Considering my ignorance about birth control, their fear was justified.

They would have been devastated had I become pregnant before marriage. Faced with choosing risk of pregnancy or marriage at a too-young age, they agreed to a June wedding. In fact, they never explicitly gave me their approval, but simply didn't protest. They were less than enthusiastic.

Across the river in Natchez, Richard's parents didn't appear to be the least bit concerned about our ages of sixteen and twenty, especially Rita. Her big smile was accompanied hearty congratulations, and followed by offer to help make wedding plans. For a fleeting moment, a look passed over Ed's face that made me wonder if he knew something he wasn't saying. But the look passed quickly, and he joined in our small celebration.

Chapter 7

Who Are You Again?

April 1961

"How about June fourth, the first week after school's out?" Richard and I studied the calendar.

"No, I need one more week."

"June eleventh?"

"Mmm. All right."

"Okay, I've done my part." He smiled with a mock smugness. "Everything else is up to you."

Initially, the excitement of wedding planning grabbed all my attention. The event itself was all I thought about, not the months and years to follow. Still in that hazy time of "the future," the wedding didn't even seem altogether real. It was indistinct, like an amorphous dream.

~~~~~~

As Richard and I looked at the assortment of engagement rings and wedding bands, I had mixed feelings. I was glad I was selecting the ring myself, one that suited my taste because, after all, I would wear it for a lifetime. Even so, part of me regretted the lack of a surprise, romantic proposal, complete with ring. Nevertheless, buying an engagement ring made the impending wedding more real.

"I plan to spend about five hundred dollars," Richard boasted to the gentleman behind the counter, not realizing that amount limited the purchase to only a small diamond. Even as we were led to the lower-priced selections, I was flattered he would spend that much. A single, small diamond suited me; I didn't care for the fancier, ornate designs with more or larger stones. Mother had taught me well to avoid anything the least bit showy; we were worthy of only the most modest things. I chose a small, flawed solitaire diamond with a plain wedding band to match. I couldn't see the flaw without the jeweler's loupe, so what difference did it make? I didn't deserve a perfect stone anyway.

The wedding plans were limited by calendar and cost. Even if I had wanted something more elaborate, we didn't have time to put together anything more than a simple wedding. My parents' budget presented an equal constraint.

Even if they had been able to afford more, spending a lot of money on any event that lasted only a few hours—even a wedding—seemed wasteful. I had no taste for a big party. My strict religious, conservative upbringing caused me to view a wedding as a solemn, holy occasion. A small, low-cost affair seemed appropriate.

The location was never in doubt—The Sevier Memorial Methodist Church, the church my dad had helped found many years earlier, and the church I had attended all my life. We decided on a Sunday afternoon ceremony, followed by a brief, casual reception at my house. Mother took charge of flowers for the church and the refreshments for the reception; my primary task was to choose a dress. I decided on the simplicity of a plain, short white dress sewn by a friend. I didn't need an elaborate wedding gown.

We decided we wanted only one attendant each. A small wedding called for a small wedding party. Choosing my attendant was easy—I only wanted a maid of honor, and that would, of course, be Susan. She had been my constant friend since third grade.

After much deliberation, Richard asked his father to be his best man. I thought it curious he didn't ask a friend. It seemed to me that he asked his dad because he had no one else. Didn't he have any friends his age who were close enough to ask? Another question I refused to think about for long.

As the date crept closer, and the wedding became reality, more doubt surfaced. The little voice in my had struggled to be heard, warning me to be sure this was what I wanted. I fought to ignore it. Voices around me were louder, most of which urged me on rather than trying to stop me. Richard grew more eager by the day, as did his parents. The prospect of my achieving full-fledged, adult status excited my friends. As Jo Ann and Marie made plans to go to college, to continue *preparation* for life, I was about to embark on my *actual* life.

In my private moments, I wondered about this person to whom I was about to commit my life. I'd seen enough to know Richard's parents were very different from mine. They both smoked and his father drank regularly and heavily, unlike anyone I had ever been around. They were the first adults I knew who placed less value on living a principled life than on making money. Not that I would characterize them as immoral, but they were less encumbered by a moral code than anyone else I had known. They often spoke of "bending" rules. For example, Rita described how she cleverly cheated on their taxes. And I'd started to glimpse that I'd surely be marrying not only Richard, but his family, too.

In spite of those concerns, I lacked the courage to admit I had been hasty. I couldn't give up my dream of becoming Mrs. Richard Walker, a married woman. Once the plan was in motion, I lacked the mettle to interrupt the momentum. Not only must I follow through with the marriage, but I must make it work—to show them all I knew what I was doing.

Chapter 8

This is No Fairy Tale

The big day brought nervousness on multiple levels.

We had decided to forgo a rehearsal. Susan had recently moved away to Memphis and was scheduled to arrive in town late Saturday evening, the night before the ceremony. With so few of us in the wedding party, the minister assured us he could guide us through the ceremony with no rehearsal. I wasn't so confident.

As I worked on my hair and makeup, the voice of doubt whispered in my ear once again.

What if Mr. Lincoln and Mr. Loomis were right? Am I doing the right thing? Who is this person I'm about to marry?

Not all of the voices had encouraged me to get married so young. Soon after I announced my intentions, Mr. Loomis, my high school principal, invited me to his office and tried to get me to reconsider. "Are you sure about this? I hope you realize what a commitment marriage is. I really wish you'd wait until after you graduate."

"I appreciate your concern, but I've thought it through, and I'm sure. We're really in love."

"Well, if you insist on going through with this, I want you to promise me one thing. Promise you'll stay in school and graduate. I'll stand behind you every way I can during the next year. Just promise me you won't drop out."

"I promise, Mr. Loomis. I'll graduate with my class."

Two days later, Mr. Lincoln, the band director—and also the choir director at my church—largely repeated the same line of reasoning Mr. Loomis had used. Once he could see I was not likely to change my mind, he asked me to make the same commitment to stay in school.

Now, hair and makeup complete, I put on my simple white dress and white shoes. Staring at my reflection in the mirror, I wondered just for an instant if I should have listened more carefully to Mr. Loomis and Mr. Lincoln. The thought was moved aside by Mother's voice. "Come on, Bettie. It's time to leave for the church."

When Mother, Daddy and I arrived at the church, the minister's wife led us to an empty room in the back. We were told Richard and his family were already there and waiting in a nearby room.

When Susan arrived moments later, she looked as nervous as my insides felt. Just as I had never been a bride, she had never been a bridesmaid. She had never even attended a Protestant wedding. Susan was Jewish. I had been to Friday night services with her at her temple a few times; she had attended church with me on Sunday mornings on several occasions. But she had never seen a Christian wedding, just as I had never seen a Jewish wedding. I could only imagine how nervous I would have been to be *in* a Jewish wedding.

After she and I greeted each other, I tried to reassure her that the minister promised he would guide us through the ceremony. Apparently the ceremony wasn't her only concern. I saw in her large, sable eyes the same doubt that lurked in the back of my head. Her mouth resisted the smile she tried to force on it, but instead joined the rest of her face in a questioning look.

"Are you sure you want to go through with this, Bettie?" she whispered.

What could I say? I wasn't about to change my mind when people were coming into the church at that very moment. And then there were all those wedding presents I had received.

Just four weeks earlier, Mother had come home from work positively beaming after learning that twelve women were giving me a wedding shower. In our church community, most wedding showers were hosted by four to six women. I knew that the large number of hostesses was a tribute to my parents, not to me. Daddy had worked in the only local hardware store in town for twenty years, and Mother had worked as a nurse at the only hospital in the area for almost as long. And they had been active members of our church longer than that. Between them, they knew most of the people in the area. Still, twelve hostesses thrilled Mother.

At the shower, the food had seemed extravagant and gifts of china, crystal, sterling silverware, fruit bowls, mixers, toasters, sheets, towels, blankets, etc., were all so much more than I expected. I knew that the giving of a wedding present doesn't necessarily signify approval of the union itself. Some of the gifts were from friends of my parents who didn't even know me—or that I was only sixteen. Yet, the shower and all those gifts somehow had bound me tighter to the commitment, and increased my determination to make the marriage work. I couldn't imagine returning all those gifts and explaining it had all been a mistake.

"Yes, Susan, I'm sure. It'll work out. You'll see."

"Oh, Bettie, I hope so. I really do want you to be happy."

Jo Ann, Marie, and Mary Beth came in, too. They shared little of Susan's concern. Their wide-eyed faces and giggles expressed unrestrained enthusiasm.

Soon the minister came and announced, "It's time."

Jo Ann, Marie, and Mary Beth accompanied Mother around the outside to the sanctuary entrance. Daddy, Susan, and I waited a bit before following them, stopping outside the main doors.

Muscles twitched of their own accord. My throat was dry. My skin tingled. Susan, no more composed than I, complained of sweaty hands.

The three of us stood together listening for Susan's musical signal. When we heard it, Susan entered nervously. Daddy closed the big door after her. He turned and smiled, his blue eyes sparkling with a little extra moisture. "Well, Bet, I guess this is it. Thank goodness you're not going to be an old maid. Whew!" He pretended to wipe his brow. His humor eased my nervousness a little.

His face softened as tears collected on his lower eyelids. "I know you're about to become a married woman, but remember you'll always be my little girl." He kissed me on the cheek, then pulled out a handkerchief and dabbed his eyes.

He handed me another handkerchief for my own eyes and my about-to-drip nose. Just for an instant, I wanted to cling to Daddy and not go through with the wedding.

We listened. My heart pounded. My face flushed.

Oh, God, please help me get through this. And please tell me I'm doing the right thing.

Then we heard it. Dum-dum-da-dum.

It's time. No turning back now.

Daddy opened the heavy door. The church was filled—many more people than I expected. Most of them were looking right at me. My stomach quivered. My shaky legs were able to take me down the aisle only because Daddy steadied me with his arm.

I looked ahead to see Richard, his eyes sparkling. He didn't look nervous at all. His wide smile proclaimed only eagerness and self-assurance. Approaching him, I wished I could absorb some of his calmness and confidence.

Suddenly time stretched and warped. The minister's voice sounded far away, and was nearly drowned out by the blood pumping in my ears.

My demeanor revealed the uncertainty I felt as I made solemn promises that day. I didn't once look at Richard as I vowed to love and to cherish him. My gaze remained locked on the minister, as if he could erase all the doubt wrenching my gut, and somehow ensure the success of the marriage. Later, Mother said my voice was so low she wondered if I had really said anything at all.

When the minister concluded the brief ceremony by saying, "You may kiss the bride," I finally turned to Richard. He gave me a quick kiss and then grabbed by hand and we turned to face our guests. I forced a nervous, timid smile as we walked down the aisle. Once outside, Richard gave me another kiss and big hug. "We're married, Bet." He seemed so excited.

"Yes, we are." His enthusiasm and happiness was contagious. My nervousness faded, and my sense of time gradually returned to normal.

It was over and done. We rushed to Richard's nearby car. Inside the car and alone, Richard kissed me and held my hand. Seeing his broad smile, I remembered why I was there. Suddenly, relief and happiness flooded through me. Driving to my house for the reception, we giggled that we were officially husband and wife. Richard kept calling me Mrs. Richard Walker.

During the reception, Richard fidgeted, shifting his weight from one leg to the other, as we greeted person after person. Fortunately, I knew most of the people there. Very few of Richard's friends had attended and he had no extended family nearby, so he knew very few of the people there. He looked as if he wanted to bolt from the room.

As soon as the last guest had been greeted, Richard pulled me aside and whispered in my ear, "Let's get out of here. The car's ready to go."

"But we can't leave yet. We haven't cut the cake, and we have to throw the bouquet and garter. Besides, these people are here to celebrate with us. It would be rude to leave now."

With an impatient sigh, he said, "Then let's go ahead and do all that stuff. I want to leave soon." Even though I wanted to please Mother and the guests by staying longer, pleasing Richard was more important. I stalled him as long as I could before I whispered to Mother that we were ready to cut the cake.

She looked disappointed we were in such a hurry, but she gathered everyone around. Richard eagerly ate the cake I offered to him, and then, in a rush, nearly forced a piece into my mouth. Soon after that, I threw the bouquet to the few single females. Then he took off my garter and tossed it, although there were no single men there.

When we went to my bedroom for me to change into traveling clothes, Richard wanted us to escape out of the bedroom window to make a fast getaway. I refused. I knew how disappointed the guests would be if they were deprived of the departure tradition.

We said quick goodbyes, ran through the traditional shower of rice, and set out to face our new life.

Our honeymoon was as brief and economical as the wedding itself—three days at the Holiday Inn in Natchez. Richard had been in charge of that, and it was apparent that he had put out little effort. No flowers in our room, no romantic plans. Just that we were staying in a hotel room as husband and wife.

Sadly, the only memorable part of that stay was dinner on our wedding night. Richard ordered medium rare filet mignons for both of us. He assured me I would like it. Because my family shopped on a limited budget, I had never had a choice cut before. I hesitated at the first bite, but was quickly delighted—I can still remember its delectable flavor and a tenderness I never knew existed. My taste in food became much more expensive that evening.

The remainder of the honeymoon was remarkable only in its blandness; no other details have survived in my memory.

At the small dinette table in our tiny apartment, I sat writing "thank you" notes. It was mid-morning on the fifth of July. Nearing the end of the card list, I had long since grown tired of writing the same phrases over and over.

Your gift was so thoughtful. I'm sure we'll enjoy it for years to come. How sweet of you to think of us in such a thoughtful way.

Not that I didn't sincerely feel the words on each card, but I kept imagining an embarrassing image of people comparing notes and discovering they were all the same.

While I wrote, I tried not to think back over the weekend, because when I did, my handwriting became shakier. Richard had started celebrating on Sunday and continued right through to the Fourth of July on Tuesday. He missed work on Monday because he stayed out too late and drank too much Sunday night. I worried about him calling in sick on the Monday before a holiday, but he assured me the company expected a lot of people to be out and didn't mind.

What bothered me the most, though, was the transformation as he drank. In my sheltered life, I hadn't been around anyone who had more than a glass of wine, or an occasional beer. My parents didn't drink at all. About the only people I had been around who drank were Susan's parents. But their alcohol consumption was infrequent and minimal. Her mother sometimes had a glass of wine after dinner, and once in a while her dad had a beer on the weekend.

Richard had gone out drinking with his friends a few times before, but by the time I saw him, he was either very tired and sleepy, or suffering from a hangover the next morning. This was the first time I was with him while he was drinking.

Sunday was spent at the lake, boating and picnicking. With each beer, Richard's cockiness and sarcasm increased. He turned into a stranger—not the person I fell in love with. I wanted to leave, but lacked the courage to say so. I pretended to have fun, lest I upset him.

I even told myself I was the abnormal one, the one out of step. After all, isn't this the way most people live? Isn't it normal to drink in celebration of our nation's birthday, or one's own birthday, or any of myriad special occasions? I even started to blame my parents for my lack of exposure to the way most people lived. Clearly, I was the one who needed to ease up and not be so critical.

None of those thoughts took the knot out of my stomach, though.

~~~~~~~

When the last thank-you note was written, I joyfully put the gift cards away in a keepsake box, leaving our small dinette table clear for the first time. The tiny, furnished apartment, situated in the landlord's backyard, had been constructed for use as a mother-in-law suite. The intended occupant had since passed on, and it had been converted to a rental. In spite of its limited space, we thought it was perfect for our first, very own apartment.

Consisted of only three rooms, its only outside door opened directly into the combination bedroom/sitting room. An archway on the right led to the small kitchen/dining area, with a small bathroom carved out in between.

The wedding presents that we didn't have room for or couldn't use yet—and there were many—were boxed and stacked near the front door, destined for storage at my parents' house. We barely had enough room for the things we needed daily. We could do without the fine china and a pink fruit bowl that was more decorative than functional.

Marie and I had always enjoyed visiting while driving casually around the area, so she offered to take me and the boxes out to the farm while we chatted. When she asked me how married life was going, I carefully avoided any mention of Richard's drinking, or of his having missed work on Monday. We were very happy, thanks for asking, and I loved being married.

I couldn't possibly allow anyone to see that cracks were already forming in my perfect, carefully-thought-out married life.

～～～

Richard and I enjoyed the next few weeks, playing our parts in our little happy-ever-after world. But then Richard missed work again because of another hangover, and I worked overtime to quiet the little voice in my head. I busied myself with cooking, cleaning, and doing laundry—and being abidingly supportive of my husband, as every good wife should. The only voice I was willing to heed was the voice of determination.

This marriage will work. I will see to it. Nothing will interfere.

Chapter 9
Don't Worry. It'll be All Right

September 1961

I shut off the alarm's rude shriek. The clock read six thirty. *What day is it? Oh, it's Monday. School. Work.*

The return to school had ended my summer of leisure, although getting up at this hour was nothing new for me. Throughout the summer, I had taken Richard to work many days so I could have the car. Even on the days I didn't take him, I still got up so that I could make him breakfast and pack his lunch.

Waking up early was not easy for Richard, however. I pushed on his shoulder. "Wake up, honey. It's time to go to work."

"Uh-uh. Leave me alone."

"Come on, Richard. It's time to get up." Richard rarely responded to an alarm. I had learned this soon after the wedding, and had assumed the duty of getting him out of bed and off to work. More than once I wondered who had done that for him before we were married.

He squirmed further under the covers and pulled the pillow over his head. Another shake elicited only more groans. Finally he mumbled, "Call in sick for me, Bet. I can't make it to work today."

If the morning-after smell of alcohol was any gauge, he had good reason to be suffering a dandy of a hangover. But it was no excuse for missing work—again.

The day before, he had gone boating with friends. I waited up for him until around midnight, when I gave up and went to bed.

He had stumbled in after two. I wasn't surprised that now, only a few hours later, he didn't feel like going to work.

I didn't want to make the phone call for him. I didn't want to lie and say he was sick when he was really suffering with a hangover. But as an obedient wife, I took a deep breath and dialed. I knew why I hadn't wanted to make the call when his boss shouted, "Tell him not to bother coming back. He's fired. We don't need people who can't show up for work."

Fired?

"Richard, guess what? Apparently, they *do* care if you miss work too much. You've just been *fired.*"

He barely groaned.

Why isn't he upset? He just lost his job?

Stunned, I showered and dressed for school. He could miss work and get fired if he wanted to, but I was not going to miss school. By the time I was ready to leave, he was half awake.

"Richard, aren't you the least bit upset? You've just been fired. What are we going to do?"

"Don't worry, Bet. We'll be okay." The job with Johns-Manville, a large manufacturing plant in Natchez, hadn't been anything exceptional. It was entry-level, but it was a decent enough blue-collar job for a kid with only a high school education, and offered an opportunity for advancement.

"How can you be so calm? How do you think we're going to pay the bills and have enough to eat with no paycheck? Where are you going to get another job as good as that one?"

"Don't get so excited. Everything's under control. I have a plan."

"What plan?"

"Don't worry about it. We'll be all right, you'll see."

"Well, I'm going to school. At least one of us can do what we're supposed to," I said under my breath.

There was no good-bye kiss.

It was difficult to pay attention in my classes that day because "He's fired" kept echoing in my brain. Either Richard truly wasn't worried, or he was a good pretender. And the little voice of doubt, which I had worked so hard to keep out of my thoughts, was back—and loud this time.

Who is this person who can't get up, who gets fired for missing too much work? Why doesn't he understand how important it is to be dependable? What's going to happen to us?

When I got home from school, I expected to find he had spent the day looking for another job. He hadn't.

"Don't rush me, Bet. I need a few days to rest. I don't know why you're in such a panic anyway."

Dirty dishes littered the small kitchen, crumpled clothes lay on the floor, and newspaper cluttered the unmade bed.

"Look at this place. The least you can do is clean up your own mess."

His idea of cleaning was to move the dirty dishes from the table to the sink, and kick his dirty clothes and towel into the corner of the bathroom. He did manage to pick up the newspaper.

I washed the dishes and straightened the bathroom and bedroom.

This continued through the week, until we went to visit his parents on Saturday. They had been expecting us to come over for dinner. We hadn't been there long when his mother asked, "How's the job going, son?"

Richard quickly responded, "Fine."

I gave him a sharp look, which his mother noticed. She raised her eyebrows at him, prompting him to say, "I don't have my job any more. I got fired."

His father's face turned red and his hands balled into fists. Punching the air, he said, "Damn it, Richard, how could you get yourself fired? That was a good job. When are you going to grow up and be a man?"

In contrast, his mother remained calm. "I'm sorry you lost your job, son, but don't worry. It'll be all right."

I noticed she didn't say *got fired*, but *lost your job*, as if it wasn't his fault, as if he deserved sympathy. Her cryptic expression tried to disguise her reaction, but I thought I saw something akin to pleasure just under the surface.

Rita was an attractive woman, tall and thin, with high cheekbones and gleaming green eyes, which complemented her tan skin and long, thick hair. Born and raised in West Texas, she claimed to be part Native American, and she certainly looked it. Her personality and ramrod straight posture exemplified the grit often attributed to Texas women. She exercised a vice-like control over the men in her life: Ed, Richard, and his younger brother Robert.

Rita was striking when she wore make-up and nice clothes and styled her hair. But just as often she appeared as unkempt as a bag lady—no makeup, loose hair falling limp and stringy, and clothes that had come from a thrift store years before and still refused to match or fit properly. She cycled unpredictably from one extreme to the other. From either mood, though, she wielded her will over the family.

I hadn't been in the family long when I heard a story that gave me a great deal of insight into the strength of her will. When Richard was about five, Rita discovered Ed was carrying on an affair with a younger woman. Not to be outdone by this, Rita moved the young woman into their home and told Ed, "Sleep with her all you want, just don't tell anyone." Holding her head high, Rita told people that the woman was their live-in housekeeper. Rita made it clear to Ed that she intended to remain married to him for the remainder of her natural life, and a mere affair was not going to interfere with her plans.

Rita had a remarkable talent. Each time she recalled past events, the story changed slightly so that with each telling the story was closer to what she wished it had been. Over time, she somehow convinced herself the skewed version was true. I learned not to trust the complete accuracy of her accounts of the past.

Ed was a man beaten down both by his own weaknesses and by Rita's control. Years of heavy drinking had given him a ruddy skin color, swollen nose, paunchy stomach, and shaky hands. For hours at a stretch, his body conformed to his favorite chair at the end of the kitchen table, where his wistful eyes looked out the window. I was never quite sure if he was looking into the future or into the past, but he gave me the clear impression he didn't want to be in the present. Coffee started Ed's day and beer ended it, with a steady supply of cigarettes throughout.

In spite of his own dissipation, he wanted to hold Richard accountable for his actions, but Rita held the power. Her words urged Richard to grow up and be responsible, but her actions said she wanted him to be forever dependent on her.

In her sincere-but-twisted effort to raise her sons as she thought best, she made conflicting demands. In spite of Ed's womanizing and heavy drinking, she defended him to the boys and demanded they respect him. At the same time, she condemned those same behaviors, especially the drinking, to the boys. I eventually concluded it would have taken many years of therapy to unravel the effects of her ambiguous messages.

~~~~~~

Rita's solution for Richard's sudden lack of a job, with no challenge from Ed, was to bring him back to work in the family business. "We need to hire another person anyway. Why work for someone else when you can work for us?"

A chemical engineer, Ed worked for a chemical company that specialized in analyzing crude oil and prescribing the chemical treatment required to make it pipeline-ready. Oil comes out of the ground in wide range of consistencies, from nearly as thin as gasoline the as thick and heavy syrup. It can also contain a variety of impurities.

Ed went from well to well, taking samples of the crude oil, performing various tests on it, and determining the proper treatment. Crude oil is usually treated with a combination of chemicals or heating, or a combination of the two. Since Ed was familiar with many oil field sites in the area, he knew the condition of the storage tanks, and what kind of treatment the contents of those tanks require.

This led the Walkers to create a second business of their own—cleaning the bottoms of these oil storage tanks. Often the crude was heavy and sometimes contained a lot of paraffin, which made it too thick to flow easily. Periodically, these tanks needed to have the accumulated sludge cleaned from the bottoms. A two-man team was used—one to crawl inside the tank and push the sludge to the pump intake, the other to stay outside and operate the pump. The outside man was also there for safety, in case the inside man fell or was overcome with fumes. The work was dirty, but not so difficult, and it paid well enough.

The Walkers' business was a perfect companion to Ed's job, which provided him the contacts in the oil business. Also, because Ed was a chemical engineer, he had the means to treat the salvaged oil and get it pipeline ready, so he could sell it. He didn't charge for cleaning the tanks; his payoff came in the sale of the reclaimed oil.

Richard had started helping in the business years before, but had left for the job at Johns-Manville. The Walkers had recently lost a worker, so with Richard now unemployed, Rita grabbed the opportunity to fill the opening.

As soon as we were alone, I said, "Richard, I don't think it's a good idea to work for your parents. I think it's better to keep your job separate from family."

"But, Bet, I've worked for them before, and it was fine. They need me, and it's better than them having to go out and hire a stranger."

"I don't know. I've heard it's not good to mix business and family."

I didn't yet understand the extent to which Rita coddled and manipulated her son, even if he was now twenty-one years old. Nor did I understand that Richard didn't really want to cut the cord that tied him so closely to Rita.

I lost the argument.

Chapter 10

Best Christmas Ever?

Richard's first act in his new job was to draw an advance. When I saw the looks exchanged between mother and son, I knew why he hadn't been worried the day he got fired. He knew his mother would give him both money and a job.

Rita decided we should live closer to them. With no regard for my distance from school—or that I'd be not merely outside the school district, but in another *state*—she located a house for us in Natchez. In order to make the move more appealing, Rita gave us what she called a late wedding present—a few pieces of "starter furniture." Even though it was used and showing its age, it nevertheless looked beautiful to me. Blond mahogany, it included a complete bedroom and tables for the living room. We bought a small dinette, and my mother donated an old sofa to round out minimal furnishings.

The house sat on a hill about a hundred yards from the house occupied by Richard's new co-worker, Joel. In his early thirties, married and father of three, Joel stayed out drinking more evenings than he went home to his family. His wife, Christine, fended for herself and their small children as best she could with the meager amount of money Joel brought home.

Richard thought the house and location were great. "It'll be so convenient for me to be closer to work, Bet. Joel and I can ride together so you can have the car for school, and we can be friends with Joel and Christine. It'll be great. You'll see."

I swallowed my doubts about living so close to someone who did not appear to be a positive influence for Richard, and set to work. Empty, the small, dirty cinderblock house gave off no cheer. Its hard tile floors echoed every sound, and the numerous jalousie windows refused to seal. I cleaned the house, and added a few rugs and wall hangings for warmth. I did my best to revive the furniture by rubbing it with furniture wax before I arranged it. By the time we were settled, I had quieted the little voice of concern once more. Richard admired my efforts, confirming that everything would be all right. It just had to be.

In our new environment, I was sure I could influence Richard to be more responsible and drink less. His mother apparently believed this, too. About this time Rita confided she had encouraged Richard to marry me, hoping my influence would have a settling effect on him—as if I would somehow redeem him. I felt flattered and up to the task. I couldn't yet see that I had been sucked into the powerful Walker family vortex, helpless to resist Rita's influence just as much as Richard's.

Small towns do have their advantages. Principal Loomis overlooked the fact that I now resided in another state, and quietly advised me to use my parents' address for school purposes. I continued in school as usual, even though my daily commute was much longer.

~~~~~~

Right alongside my determination to improve Richard stood my determination to be graduated with my class. Too many people—including Mr. Loomis and Mr. Lincoln—had expressed doubt I would stick with school. I had to show them, just as I had to show them my marriage would work. I worked hard at both tasks.

Rita continued to occasionally advance us money for necessities, but she refused to make the payments on the boat. When it became clear that he couldn't afford it—he was three months behind on the payments—she insisted Richard let it go back. Richard protested loudly, but she won out in the end and he returned the boat. I secretly applauded that his mother finally did something I agreed with. In my opinion, the boat had only provided him an excuse to go out and drink with his friends. Without that, we would be much better off.

December 1961

"Hey, Bet, let's go shopping for a Christmas tree."

"Really? You want to go buy a tree?" Until then, he had shown little interest in anything either domestic or holiday-related. I was excited that he wanted to take an active role in preparing for Christmas.

"Yeah, sure I do."

A few minutes later, we pulled into a tree lot and looked around. "How about this one?" I held out the limbs of a small tree. I didn't think we could afford a larger tree. Besides, we had no decorations, so I was thinking of the expense of enough to cover a larger tree.

"Oh, that one's too little. How about one of these big ones over here?"

Ignoring my protests, Richard paid for the tree and headed off to the car with it over his shoulder. He then went back and picked up a few pieces of discarded greenery to use for making a wreath.

In the car, he swelled with pride. "Now we need decorations for our first Christmas tree."

"Well, when my brother left home, my parents let him take a few of his favorite decorations. Maybe they'll let me do the same thing."

"Okay, let's go."

With Mother's permission, I raided her tree ornaments. I chose a set of seven small metal bells, a plastic angel tree topper, and a few other assorted items. We then headed to Richard's parents, where he took a few glitter-covered balls and other vintage glass ornaments. On the way home, we bought a tree stand, two inexpensive boxes of ornaments, a couple of multi-colored light strings, and a package of icicles.

Richard convinced the tree to stand straight in the stand, and then he helped me decorate it. He even helped me fashion a wreath for the front door with the extra greenery. After we finished, we sat sipping hot chocolate and gazing at our very first Christmas tree. I *did* like it. I had put aside concerns over money after Richard said several times, "It's Christmas, Bet."

He squeezed my hand. "This'll be the best Christmas I ever had. Our first Christmas married. And I know what I'm getting you, too. You'll be so surprised." He winked as he gently poked me in the ribs.

"Careful, you'll make me spill my hot chocolate... and I know what I'm getting you, too. I can't wait. Let's open our gifts to each other here, just the two of us."

"Yeah, let's do." He put his arm around me and squeezed.

Yes, this will be the happiest Christmas ever.

~~~~~~

Early in the afternoon on the day before Christmas Eve, we went to visit the Walkers. After coffee and chit-chat, Richard stood and announced, "I'm going out Christmas shopping. I'll be back in a little while."

Rita and I wrapped gifts and baked Christmas cookies. By six o'clock, Rita remarked, "Richard sure is taking his time with his shopping. He must have gone to the North Pole." In a town as small as Natchez, shopping shouldn't take long.

"He'd better be buying something spectacular, as long as it's taking," I said, as optimistically as I could. In truth, I was angry at having been abandoned. Seven o'clock came and still no Richard. Weary of waiting, we ate dinner without him. After dinner, we sat at the kitchen table playing Gin Rummy. Smothered by the cigarette smoke that filled the room—both Rita and Ed smoked—I yearned to go home.

At ten o'clock, we gave up on the cards and retreated to the living room to watch the news on TV. By ten thirty, worry and anger battled for priority in my thoughts. No stores were open past nine, and the drive home from anywhere in the area took no more than twenty minutes.

"He probably ran into some old friends and lost track of time," Rita said. Her taut face didn't match her optimistic words, however. Ed's attention remained intently focused on the TV, his face showing no expression.

To keep my rising anger at bay, I tried to believe the most likely reason for the delay was car trouble of some kind, maybe a flat tire. I hoped he hadn't been in an accident. I knew Rita and Ed were thinking of trouble, too, but I suspected they had in mind trouble of a different sort.

Ed went to bed around eleven thirty. Rita made a fresh pot of coffee. She shoved cigarettes at me and poured me coffee, making it clear that I should stay up—as a *dutiful* wife should. Around one thirty, the ringing phone shattered the quiet of the wee hours.

Rita answered. "Hello...You're where?...What are the charges?... I'll be right there...Okay, then I'll be there at six sharp."

Richard had been arrested on a DUI charge.

Arrested!

Like a tidal wave, anger welled up inside me.

How could he do this to me? He left me here so he could go out drinking. Did he even intend to go shopping?

With cheeks afire, my jaws tightened and my hands clenched into fists. Only my overriding desire to please Rita prevented me from voicing my anger and humiliation.

Instead, I forced my fists open and dropped my jaw. With a tight but controlled voice, I said, "Maybe if he has to stay in jail a day or two, he won't make the same mistake again."

Ed appeared in the doorway; he had been awakened by the phone. "What's going on?"

Rita answered, "Richard's been arrested."

Ed's face turned a deeper crimson than usual. Through clenched teeth, and punching the air with a fist, he said, "Let him sit there. It'll teach him a lesson. I don't want him to expect us to bail him out every time he gets himself into trouble."

Rita ignored Ed. Straightening her back even more, raising her head another notch, she pronounced, "We can't let him sit in jail over Christmas. That's no way for a family to spend the holiday. I'm going down first thing in the morning and get him out."

Ed shook his head in disgust, turned around, and went back to bed.

The decision made, I decided to get some sleep on the Walkers' living room sofa. I hadn't yet discovered the value of staying awake all night, as Rita apparently had. During any crisis, she not only stayed awake—or at least she said she did—but also wore her lack of sleep like a badge of honor.

The next morning, the opening of the back door woke me. I stretched out the kinks as Rita and Richard walked into the living room, Richard empty handed. Just as I suspected, he had not made it to even one store.

His head drooped and he averted his eyes to avoid looking directly at me. Groggy, I let him speak first. He knelt beside the sofa and launched into his apology, which flowed like honey. "Bet, I'm so sorry. You have every right to be angry. I know I was wrong. I just stopped to have one beer and I don't know what happened. I promise it won't ever happen again. Please say you'll forgive me."

I looked from him to Rita, who hovered nearby. Even though my anger resurfaced, pressure to please Richard and his parents overrode my temptation to express it. Instead, I spoke the words I knew Rita wanted to hear, although with a distinct lack of enthusiasm. "Okay, I forgive you." Rita's slight nod signaled her approval.

Richard continued, "Oh, Bettie, I'm gonna straighten up and fly right. You'll see."

I wanted to leave the Walkers' immediately and forget the entire, humiliating incident. After all, this wasn't our normal life, but only an aberration. I wanted to blot out the whole thing and just get back to our holiday plans. Richard made that easy when he assured me it would never happen again. And I believed him.

We went home and proceeded as if nothing had happened. We simply skipped over our own gift exchange, which we had planned to be just between us anyway. We showed up at my family's on Christmas morning and went back to Richard's parents' Christmas afternoon. Not a word was mentioned about the previous day's events.

Chapter 11
Yes, It's Time

The new year brought more episodes of excessive drinking, most of the time with Joel, Richard's new drinking buddy. After each binge, I desperately wanted to believe Richard when he pleaded, "I'm so sorry. Oh, Bet, if you'll help me, I promise I'll quit. Please forgive me."

Believing I *could* actually help, I agreed each time. I didn't speak about these events to anyone outside our families, because these occurrences weren't a part of our actual life. Merely occasional anomalies. I treated Richard even kinder than usual, believing that if I could show him how very much I loved him and how sincerely I forgave him, he would respond by behaving better. He would have to love me back enough to control himself.

June 1962

My second semester grades reflected my conflicting roles as student and wife. I missed school on days when no one else was available, and the Walkers insisted I go with Richard on jobs, with no regard for the consequences of missing school. On the days I did attend school, I went home to keeping house and preparing dinner, studying only if I had time. Though my grades that semester were the worst ever, I still met the requirements for graduation and obtained earned my high school diploma.

With school behind me, I focused exclusively on being a good wife, putting an emphasis on "helping" Richard. Putting distance between us and Joel seemed as if it would reduce Richard's temptation. I used the pretense of wanting to be nearer my family and friends to suggest we move back to Louisiana. Richard agreed to the move and Rita didn't resist. I reckoned that by that time, Rita also recognized that our proximity to Joel had been ill-conceived. The combination of working with and living so close to Joel was just too much temptation for Richard.

We rented a small house in a subdivision near my family's farm, between Ferriday and Natchez. Unlike the one in Natchez, this house and the surrounding neighborhood projected an atmosphere of middle-class families and friendly neighbors. Cleaning, decorating, cooking, and crafts occupied my time on the days I didn't go to work with Richard. We made it to August—two whole months—with no major incidents. By this time, I had come to accept the minor ones as ordinary.

After all, it's normal for a man to stop on payday to have a few beers, isn't it? It's been a long time since Richard spent his entire check, and he hasn't gotten into another accident or been arrested. The separation from Joel has helped. Richard realizes he was drinking too much, and now he's controlling it better. We're gonna be fine.

Late August 1962

"You have a cyst on your ovary, but it's not serious. This prescription should do the trick." Dr. Gibson, for whom my mother had worked since I was six years old, smiled and patted my hand. I went to see him because my period had been late.

While I was grateful it was nothing serious, a small part of me was disappointed to learn I wasn't pregnant. For three weeks, I had been unsure. At first, I hoped I wasn't pregnant because I could just imagine the reactions. "You're too young to be having a baby." "What are you thinking?" "Don't you know what contraceptives are for?"

But as the days passed, I had warmed to the idea. We never even considered the possibility of me working; we had an unspoken understanding that we would be the traditional family of the early twentieth century—husband works, wife is mother and homemaker. Because we had been married over a year and I was out of school, it seemed like the time was right to start a family. Especially now that Richard had settled down and become more responsible.

I daydreamed about what it would be like to be pregnant, and what it would be like to have a baby, even thinking of baby names. But I wondered what Richard thought about the idea. Although he knew about the doctor's visit, we had not discussed the prospect of me being pregnant. While we were dating, we had talked about having children—but at some vague time in the future.

Now I wanted to know what he thought about starting a family. What if I had been pregnant? How would he have reacted?

To set the mood for a discussion, I made his favorite dinner: steak, baked potatoes, and salad. I carefully selected heavy, aged beef. I marinated the steak to prepare it for grilling. While the potatoes were slow-baking, I cut up greens for a salad and added tomatoes, mushrooms, carrots, and grated cheese. I had just finished setting the table when Richard came in.

"Hi, Bet. I'm home." He looked like he normally did after a day in the field—covered with oil and mud.

"Hi, honey. How was your day?"

"Long and tiring. Robert and I had two jobs. The first one was easy. The tank bottom was thin enough to pump. We didn't even have to pull the plate. But the second tank was pure paraffin, thick and gooey. We had to pull the plate, and I crawled in the tank and used a push broom to sweep the gunk over to the pump. It was so thick, the pump kept sucking air. It was slow—and dirty."

"I'm sorry it was so hard."

"I need to get out of these clothes and wash up."

"Okay. I have a steak ready for the grill."

"Hmm. You must've read my mind. I'm starving. We didn't have much with us to eat."

A half hour later, Richard cut into his steak. "This is perfect, Bet. If I listen, I can hear the steer when I cut into it." He liked his steak very rare, and I had finally learned to take it off the grill soon enough. "By the way, what did the doctor say today?"

"It's only a cyst on my ovary. He gave me a prescription that should clear it up."

"Are you sure it's nothing? Cyst sounds serious." He looked worried.

"No, he said it's fairly common. Nothing to worry about."

"I hope he's right." His face relaxed as he turned back to his plate.

After we finished eating, I asked, "Richard, how would you have reacted if I had been pregnant?"

Richard pushed his chair back. He patted his now-full stomach and smiled. He hesitated a beat before he said, "I would have been happy. I didn't say anything before because I didn't know how you felt about it, but I secretly hoped you were. I'm actually a little disappointed."

"Are you really? Are you ready for us to have a baby? Do you think it's time?"

He motioned for me to sit on his lap. "I'm ready if you are. I've been thinking about it a lot lately. I want a red-headed, freckle-faced little boy." His eyes sparkled as he laughed.

"What if it's a girl?"

"Then I'll buy her the prettiest, frilliest dresses you've ever seen." With a flirty grin, he added, "How about if we get started on this project right now?" He picked me up and carried me off to the bedroom, tickling me on the way.

Over the next few days, we fantasized about having a baby. We wondered what I would look like pregnant. We talked about diapers, bottles, and burping. I had never been around babies, and worried I wouldn't know how to take care of one. Richard assured me he knew a lot about them, telling me how he helped take care of Robert when he was a baby, along with a few others since.

Of course, neither of us could think beyond having an infant; we couldn't fathom having a child of six, or ten, or fifteen, nor could we imagine the responsibility required to raise a child to adulthood—or the cost. We were merely infatuated with the idea of playing dolls.

~~~~~

In late October, Mother dropped by to check on her pregnant daughter. She found me still in bed, even though it was late morning.

"Bettie, you look awful. You're thin and pale, and you look dehydrated. When did you bathe last?"

"A couple of days ago." My voice sounded weak.

"How long since you ate?"

"I don't remember. I've had bad morning sickness. I can't keep anything down. Every time I try to eat, I get sick."

Walking toward the kitchen, she called over her shoulder, "I'll see what I can find for you." She turned the corner. "Good gracious, Bettie! Look at this mess. How long have these dirty dishes been here?"

"I know it's bad, but I've been too sick to clean in there."

"Well, up to now, I've tried not to interfere, but this is just too much. Why hasn't Richard helped you?"

"He's been working a lot. He says he needs to work all he can because we need the money."

"I'll tell you what you need. You need to eat something. Then you need to get bathed and dressed so I can take you to the doctor. You're dangerously dehydrated and undernourished."

~~~~~

Dr. Gibson frowned. "You're severely dehydrated. You've lost eight pounds since your last visit, and you didn't have it to spare. I'll give you something for the nausea, but if you don't start keeping down more liquids, I'll need to admit you to the hospital and feed you intravenously."

Back in her car, Mother said, "You're coming home with me. Until you feel better, you can't stay in that house by yourself. You and Richard are going to stay with us for a while so your daddy and I can keep an eye on you." Under her breath, she added, "Richard sure isn't taking care of you."

Her last remark stung, mostly because I knew it was true. The more the morning sickness had worsened, the more impatient and distant Richard had become, saying what he needed to do most was work. The little voice in my head told me he was finding excuses to avoid taking care of me. Like I had done so many times before, I pushed the little voice aside. However much Richard hurt my feelings, I still couldn't admit his flaws to anyone else. I was still determined to make this marriage work, to prove I knew what I was doing. And now I had even more reason.

I didn't want to admit any of that to Mother, though, so I defended him. "That's because he's working so much. He's never been around anyone pregnant and he just doesn't understand."

"You don't have to understand much to see you need help," Mother muttered, more to herself than to me.

Richard agreed to the temporary move. When the days turned into weeks, Richard said it was silly to pay rent on a house we were not occupying, so we gave up the house and planned to stay until the baby was born.

That he agreed so easily to moving in with my parents, with not one word of protest, was one more blow to my pride. I wanted him to insist on being responsible for us. Instead, he willingly accepted help from my parents just as easily as he did from his. I kept these thoughts to myself, though, careful not to let Richard know he had disappointed me, and careful not to admit his failings to our parents. I thought the only bright side to this arrangement was that Richard wouldn't drink while we lived with my parents. He knew how strongly they disapproved of drinking.

Chapter 12

You're Where?

Morning sickness was soon eased by the medication, and within a month after the move, that phase had passed and my energy had returned.

Unfortunately, living with my parents didn't stop Richard's binges as I had expected. He continued to ask me to help him after each one. While I wasn't quite clear about what I should be doing, I started to feel as though I must be failing him somehow. His drinking must be partly my fault. Afraid any complaint would be another excuse for a binge, I kept quiet as his time away from home increased, both working and drinking.

My dad had always eaten a hot, meat-and-vegetables meal at both midday and evening. Since Mother was working days at the hospital, I assumed responsibility for cooking both lunch and dinner and doing most of the cleaning. It was the least I could do in exchange for our room and board. I didn't mind really. It made me feel grown up and responsible.

May 1963

Only a few weeks before my due date of June 21, Richard and Joel didn't come home after work. Rita and I thought it was just another of their typical binges until a full day had passed. By the third day, we were frantic. They had never been gone more than two nights in a row. Rita and I searched for them everywhere, going to every bar and honky-tonk we saw. We found no trace of them.

Dr. Gibson had already prescribed Librium, an anti-anxiety drug, for my stress. It was no match for the extreme worry, loss of appetite, and sleeplessness I endured. Staying at the Walkers' didn't help, but Rita expected me to be there during the worry times. She wanted me to share her anguish and vigilance. She offered me a steady supply of cigarettes to "calm me down."

Six long days after they went missing, Richard finally called. He and Joel were in Big Spring, Texas—nearly seven hundred miles away. In their drunken state, they had decided to go on a road trip to visit some long-lost relative of Joel's. Heaven only knows how they managed to get that far without having an accident or getting arrested.

Out of money and out of options, Richard had once again turned to his faithful rescuer "Mom, I know we've really messed up this time, and there's no excuse. But we want to come home. Please, Mom, send us enough money to get home."

While Rita never refused Richard's requests for help, she gave it on her terms. She didn't send them money out of fear they would use it to drink more. Instead, she decided *we* should go get them. I agreed, mostly because I knew she wanted the company and because I knew she expected me to go with her. Also, it was easier than being around my parents during the crisis. Not that they said or did anything to make me feel worse; but I knew they disapproved strongly and that knowledge caused me to feel humiliated.

I didn't ask Dr. Gibson's permission for the long drive. I didn't want to give him the opportunity to tell me not to go on the fourteen-hundred-mile round trip. But sitting so long at a time caused my legs and feet to swell. Thus, I needed frequent stops to walk and stretch, which made the drive take even longer than it would have normally. We left at six in the morning and arrived in Big Spring about eight that night—a fourteen-hour drive.

Upon arriving in Big Spring, we went in search of the address Richard had given his mother. At the cheap motel, we found two tired, hungover, hungry—and surprisingly sober—men.

Joel dropped his head in embarrassment. He spoke quietly, refusing to make eye contact.

Not Richard. He wasted no time launching into his apology. He became the personification of penitence, pleading for mercy and promising atonement. "Mom, Bettie, I'm so sorry. I know I really messed up this time. You have every right to be angry. I'll do anything to make it up to both of you."

Rita's lips hardly moved as she said, "We'll talk about it later. Right now, let's just get going."

Richard then turned his attention to me. He knelt beside me and took my hand. "Bet, I know I've hurt you, but I've really learned my lesson this time. I'm gonna straighten up and fly right, and I'll find some way to make it up to you. You'll see. If you'll just help me, I promise I'm gonna be the best husband and father you've ever seen. I love you, Trinkatunia. Please forgive me."

Years before, Richard had playfully dubbed me Trinkatunia. I have no idea where that name came from, but he used it when he was being playful, and also when he was trying to sweet-talk me into forgiving him.

I tried to be stern, so I didn't reply then. But I couldn't bring myself to remain so hardhearted that I could turn away from his pleas. Every time he begged for my help, I reminded myself of my marriage vows. By the end of the two-day drive home, my anger had faded. I had once again forgiven him and believed him when he said he would reform. An event of this magnitude had surely made a profound impression on him. This time he would certainly change.

~~~~~~

While we were living with my parents, Richard developed a keen interest in the farm. On days when there was no work with his parent's business, he helped my dad, who enjoyed the company as well as the assistance. I liked seeing them together; I believed if anyone could inspire change in Richard, it was Daddy.

I watched them return from a morning of mending fences. Richard's sweaty shirt and dirty hands testified to the hard work, but what struck me was how six-foot-two Richard looked up to Daddy, only five foot five. As they gulped tall glasses of ice water, Richard asked Daddy, "You think we can finish that stretch of fence today?"

"How late are you willing to work?" Daddy lifted a bushy eyebrow.

"I can work as late as you can."

"Then let's eat and get back to it." Daddy patted Richard's shoulder.

Richard's eyes reflected his admiration for Daddy, and pride in their work.

Thank you, God. He's finally growing up.

On Monday, June 10, I woke up earlier than usual. Richard was already up and out with Daddy. As I took my first few steps, I felt warm fluid dribbling down my legs. Unsure what was happening, I called Mother, who was on duty at the hospital. She said, "It sounds like your water broke. Call Dr. Gibson right away."

The nurse said to meet him at the hospital. I knew Daddy and Richard would soon return to the house for coffee, so I packed a bag and waited for them. Less than an hour later, their faces lit up like two little boys at the prospect of the baby coming. Richard hastily cleaned up, and off we went.

"Hmm, your membranes have torn slightly, allowing amniotic fluid to leak. You're obviously not in labor yet, but there's a good chance you will be soon." Dr. Gibson smiled over the rim of his glasses. "Looks like you're about to have a baby."

"What should I do?"

Removing his gloves, he said, "I'm going to admit you, and then I want you to walk the halls. Often a little exercise triggers labor."

By early afternoon, having been installed in a room, I was walking the small, u-shaped hospital from one end to the other. I felt a few light contractions from time to time, but none pronounced or regular. Richard walked with me, asking every so often if I wanted anything.

Dr. Gibson checked me again later in the afternoon. "There's no change. You might as well go back home. But let me know right away if anything happens."

Tuesday and Wednesday brought no changes. Mild contractions woke me early Thursday morning. Richard put his hand on my distended stomach. "You think today's the day?"

"Maybe. But then I thought Monday was the day, too."

"How do you feel?"

"I feel fine. Just a little tightening every so often."

"I think you should call the doctor anyway."

I didn't call for a while because I wanted to wait and see if these light contractions were a false alarm. But they kept coming at regular intervals, so three hours I decided I had better call.

Dr. Gibson asked, "How far apart are the contractions?"

"About eight minutes. And they're very mild."

"No need to come in yet, but I want you to let me know when they're four minutes apart, or if they get hard."

I convinced Richard and Daddy to get on with their regular work. They didn't go far from the house, though, checking in every hour or so. After lunch, they refused to leave the house.

By late afternoon, with Richard and Daddy anxiously pacing around me, I timed the contractions at about four and a half minutes apart and painful enough to make me catch my breath. Both men insisted we go to the hospital. Neither man was comfortable in the company of a woman in labor.

~~~~~~

"This time," **Dr. Gibson** said, after a quick examination, "you're in labor and progressing nicely. I believe now it's for real."

Richard settled me into my room and then held my hand with each contraction. Between eight and eight thirty, the contractions transitioned into hard labor. I was transferred to the delivery room, leaving Richard to pace alone.

Her shift now over, Mother joined me in the delivery room. Labor progressed rapidly, and Karen Louise was born at ten thirty, on June thirteenth. She was twenty-one inches long, but weighed only five and a half pounds—a skinny baby. Dr. Gibson concluded she was several weeks early, that we had probably miscalculated her due date. Not only was her birth weight low, but she didn't have a lot of muscle tone. In later years, I would come to believe that not only was she a few weeks early, but also my stress, smoking, and Librium contributed to her low birth weight.

Back in my room, Richard showered both Karen and me with his sweetness. The nurses had cleaned and dressed Karen and brought her to the bassinette in my room. Richard didn't hesitate to pick her up and bring her to me. His combination of delicateness and assurance with Karen surprised me; he was more at ease with her than I was. I had never even seen a newborn baby before, much less cared for one. I was hesitant when I held her. She was so thin, so fragile, I was afraid of hurting her. Richard wasn't nervous at all, though. His confidence as he held her and cooed to her caused me to relax.

If any piece of my heart hadn't already softened after the Big Spring trip, seeing Richard dressing our newborn baby, singing to her, changing her diaper, and cradling her in the crook of his arm melted away any residual anger. While I fell in love with my new baby girl, I also fell in love with her father all over again.

After we were back at home, Richard's attentiveness continued. Each time I looked at Karen, I saw a miracle—a tiny, but complete person I had created with my own body, an amazing new life. I had been forever and profoundly changed.

Richard, obviously, had been equally affected. When I saw him walking around with her on his shoulder, my heart rejoiced at his certain transformation. He was now a truly devoted husband and father.

~~~~~~

Karen was only five weeks old when Richard's gremlins returned, taking him on a bender—and then another one a couple of weeks after that. The agony in his face, almost torment, told me his sincerity was genuine each time he gave one of his penitent speeches.

Even with such well-meaning intentions, periodically something inside him snapped, as if he were hopelessly trapped in a cycle, unable to break out. In control, out of control, in control, out of control, on and on... Still, each time he promised to straighten up and fly right, my desperation to believe him, to love him into change, equaled the sincerity of his desire to change.

Chapter 13
Rescued... Sort of

My new baby consumed much of the time and energy I had previously devoted to Richard's misadventures. Outcries of anger and disappointment slowly turned into mere sighs and shrugs.

Richard often spent an entire paycheck when he went on a binge, so we seldom had enough money, even for essentials. By now I was accustomed to not having enough, and no longer hesitated to ask Rita for help. I couldn't yet see that my life was spiraling downward, that things were not getting better.

I wasn't worth much to Richard, or else he wouldn't be irresponsible and treat me badly, or so I thought. No husband would treat a good wife the way he treated me. Since I was unable to help him, I must be a failure. It didn't matter that I had never known exactly *how* to help him.

I was hardly the independent adult I thought I would be when I planned to get married so young. I regularly received money from Rita. I accepted housing from my parents. Clearly I was not living the life we had dreamed of back when Richard was trying to win my affection while we sat in our parking spot.

Since I was clearly a failure as a wife, I wondered if I would be any better mother. This fear prompted me to work even harder to do everything right, to somehow make up for having failed so far. If I could just be good enough, and not disappoint Richard, he would have no reason to drink. The pressure to be perfect, of course, merely escalated my stress and fatigue.

As Karen's newborn baby noises grew stronger and louder, my parents' house seemed to grow smaller and the walls thinner. My mother had changed jobs and was now a relief nurse at the hospital. This meant she rotated among the three shifts—two days on each. Her sleep schedule was necessarily irregular, requiring that she often had to sleep during the day. I tried to cook, clean, and care for a baby, all without disturbing Mother's sleep. She had always been a light sleeper, but now with such an inconsistent schedule, she found it even more difficult to sleep soundly. If she awakened, I knew it must have been because of me.

I kept Karen by my side night and day, so I could quiet her as quickly as possible. I anticipated feeding times. I moved painstakingly about the kitchen in near-silence, causing every task to take longer. Noisy tasks, such as laundry, were possible only while Mother was at work. Sleep came in short stretches.

Old photos taken during that time period depicted a girl I hardly recognize now, one with a haggard face, stooped shoulders, and a stingy hint of a smile. She looked more like thirty-eight than eighteen. The night I met Richard I had felt like Cinderella at the ball; now I looked and felt more like Cinderella would have looked without the fairy godmother.

But I accepted my role with little complaint because I believed I bore the full responsibility. I alone had made the choices that brought me to where I was. And so it was I who must bear the burdens. I didn't expect or want pity from anyone. If my life was hard, it was because I deserved it.

Even so, when the Walkers offered us a way to move out of my parents' home, I didn't hesitate to accept.

Karen, their first grandchild, captured their hearts completely. Seeing her at my parents' house was awkward for the Walkers. They felt they were intruding if Mother was at home and awake, and of course they didn't come at all if Mother was sleeping. At first, they visited when Mother was working, but those days were far too infrequent to suit them. Since I had no car, Rita often came to get Karen and me and took us to her house, but I never was able to stay at the Walkers' as long as Rita would have liked because I had responsibilities at home.

During one visit, Rita said, "You know, we bought that trailer a few months back to have a place to get away on the weekends. We intended to put it on a lake, and use it as a place to fish and hunt. But we haven't found a lot yet, and the trailer's still sitting empty. I know it's old and the trailer park isn't a great neighborhood, but you two are welcome to live in it until you can do better. At least you'd have some privacy."

She anxiously awaited my response. I knew she was making the offer not only to make us more comfortable, but also—and more importantly—to have Karen closer to her. The trailer park was only a few miles from her house.

I could tell she was uncertain of my reaction. I suppose she thought I might turn up my nose at such meager accommodations. She needn't have worried.

"Really? You mean it? Yes—if Richard agrees, of course." There was a time when I *would* have thought of such a home as beneath me, but my standards had relaxed considerably.

September 1963

The trailer park was in a seedy part of town. Most of the old trailers were occupied by low income, hard-working people. Little landscaping surrounded any of them, having been replaced by a generous assortment of junk and cast-offs. The Walkers' small, two-bedroom trailer showed its years of use. The once-pleasant dusty rose and white exterior had turned into dirty pink and streaked gray, splattered with rust spots and stains.

Inside, the furnishings were minimal. The brown plaid couch and chair were worn and dirty; one leg of the coffee table slanted at an unexpected angle; and the frayed beige-and-brown curtains hung unevenly. Nicks and tears marred the vinyl-covered kitchen chairs. The carpet, once beige, had become several shades of dirt and wear.

We brought few possessions of our own, and yet it was crowded. The living room furniture barely fit after it was rearranged to make room for Karen's playpen. The only way to fit her baby bed into the second bedroom was to disassemble the twin bed and lean it against the wall. The refrigerator, stove, and sink were all undersized to fit into the compact kitchen. In the tiny bathroom, linoleum curled at the edges and a musty smell hung in the air, as if water had leaked and remained standing for a time.

But the trailer offered one fine quality—privacy.

Right away I discovered the clothes washer didn't work, leaving me to do laundry—especially Karen's diapers and baby clothes—by hand. I washed small items in the tiny kitchen sink and larger ones in the bathtub. For bulky items, I depended on an occasional trip to Rita's. Winter, the rainy season, brought as many wet days as dry ones. A community clothesline was available when weather permitted; otherwise, a wooden, folding drying rack was used inside. When the drying rack was filled, the backs of kitchen chairs were pressed into service, each one holding a diaper.

Our friendliest neighbor, Willese, was no stranger to the day-to-day struggle for survival. She helped me keep my chin up through difficult days. A sturdy, boisterous woman, she was freckle-faced, with ample curly, reddish-brown hair, a quick wit, and a generous heart. She had little formal schooling, but possessed a natural wisdom and genuine goodness. Even though she didn't have much herself, it was common for her to knock on the door saying, "I just baked up this meatloaf and I thought you'd like to have some," or "I made this big cake and we'll never eat it all" or "I'm goin' down to the store. You wanna come along?" She allowed me the use of her telephone and taught me how to make the best cornbread in the world.

By this time, I had become skilled at keeping my two lives separate. When Richard was sober, we were just another hardworking family, struggling like others around us. If we managed carefully, we hoped we could have a few things in time—a telephone, a working washing machine, a car for me, a better place to live. I had long since quit dreaming beyond these basics; anything more was out of reach for us.

I was the one who chose to get married so young and—I later realized—to someone I didn't know nearly well enough.

Is this what Mr. Loomis and Mr. Lincoln were trying to warn me about when they tried to talk me out of getting married? Did they suspect my life would be this hard? And what would my friends think if they could see me in this dilapidated trailer washing diapers in the sink, wondering if Richard will come home sober or drunk?

Susan's engaged to a dentist. Jo Ann and Marie are in college. Mary Beth has completed business school and is engaged to a nice man.

My life was strikingly different from any of theirs.

Even though humiliating, this was the better of my two lives.

Each time Richard went on a binge, I was forced into my *other* life, the dark, hopeless one, the one that made me so weary I didn't think I could keep going, the one that made me want to retreat into a shell and just quit breathing. Often after one of Richard's binges, I was paralyzed for a day or two, letting myself go, letting the house go, only giving Karen the necessary care. But each time, I eventually found the spark to pick myself up and get back to work, to regain hope for something better.

This rebound phase of my roller-coaster existence usually included cleaning, washing, and cooking with a fervor, trying again to be the perfect wife and mother. I didn't know any other way to carry out my repeated pledge to help Richard.

After each binge, and Richard's apologies and intentions to be better, I returned to the pretense of a normal life, clinging to the hope that this time the promises would be kept

They never were.

Chapter 14
Time for Action

In late October, Richard and his paycheck once again went missing on a Friday night. I borrowed Willese's phone to call Rita. She came to get Karen and me to join her for the usual vigil. I left a note telling Richard where we were, on the slight chance he came home before we did.

Rita's kitchen table was our post for phase one, coffee and cigarettes our sustenance. We waited for word, hoping Richard would call, or come there. Why we hoped I don't know, because he never did. As soon as Karen was down for the night, we left her with Ed and began phase two. In this part of the ritual, we drove by bars and honky-tonks searching for Richard's truck, hoping to prevent an accident and his injury, or worse, the injury of an innocent person. We also hoped to intercept a meeting between him and the local police.

That particular night, like most, our search failed. Three hours of driving later, we returned to the Walkers' for more coffee, cigarettes, and worry. We finally napped, although Rita never admitted she slept. Richard showed up at his mother's Saturday afternoon, still a little wobbly, but sober enough to be transitioning into his apologetic phase.

One might think I'd be incensed. But the anger was turning to numbness, the sort of numbness that has no hope. The repetitiveness of his behavior was becoming more apparent. My small voice said it was unlikely the cycle would end. Another part of me was eager to forgive Richard, to get us back to the better life I wanted to be in so desperately, the one in which Richard loved me, and where there was hope for the future. I was more than willing to say, "Yes, Richard, I forgive you and I'll help you."

Rita carted us back to the trailer Saturday evening, but returned Sunday afternoon. Weary of too many weekends filled with worry and stress, Rita had decided to take action. She knew to wait until he was completely sober, but still vulnerable, before talking to him. Her back straighter than usual and her jaw sternly set, she presented a formidable power. She parked on the front half of the chair near the door, across from Richard, who slumped on the sofa with his elbows on his knees, head slightly bowed. The angle of her head, set in military erectness, spoke of her mission.

After pouring coffee for us, I sat next to Richard, on the end of the sofa nearest Karen's playpen. I watched Karen play as I listened to what Rita had to say.

"Richard, I've had about enough of your stunts. It's time to find out what's wrong with you."

Richard's head jerked up and he opened his mouth to speak. "Mom, there's nothing wrong with— "

"There must be something wrong with you because normal people don't behave like this. Normal people don't stay out all night and into the next day, and return with their entire paycheck gone. ...Do they?"

"No... I guess not..." His shoulders drooped, causing his six foot two frame to appear small and frail.

"What do you think your problem is? Is there something wrong with you medically? Or do you have a mental problem?"

His voice weak, he searched the carpet. "I don't know, Mom. I know I don't start out to get drunk."

"Well, I don't know if your problem is physical or mental, but we're going to find out. I'm taking you to see Dr. Tischer." Her resolve was conspicuous. The pampering mother had retreated, at least for the moment.

Even though I didn't believe Richard had either a medical or an emotional problem, I was grateful Rita wanted to do *something*. This was better than her usual excuses for his behavior. She had even lectured me occasionally that "it takes two to fight," holding me partly responsible for his behavior. So I was relieved to hear her say the problem was his. Maybe her doctor would offer something to help him.

The small, shabby building was crowded. Most of those waiting appeared poor, needy, and uneducated. Rita had spoken of Dr. Tischer in glowing terms. But as I looked at the surroundings, I wondered if he was a competent doctor with the generosity to dedicate himself to caring for the indigent, or were these the only kind of people who had confidence in him?

When Richard's name was called, Rita gave me a look that said, "Stay put." She stood and went with him.

This is just like her, still treating us both like children. She's probably speaking for him, too, no doubt. Even if Richard had intended to speak candidly with the doctor, he surely won't in his mother's presence.

When they emerged, Rita said Dr. Tischer had performed some tests and it would be several days before the results were available. Richard remained close-mouthed and looked out the window.

A week later, Dr. Tischer said the tests didn't reveal anything wrong medically. He concluded a chemical imbalance caused Richard's reaction to alcohol. He recommended Richard simply not drink at all, and if he found that too difficult to do on his own, he should turn to counseling for help.

In spite of my initial skepticism about Dr. Tischer, I did like his recommendation. Maybe now Richard would realize he simply couldn't drink. After all, many people lived quite full and happy lives without drinking. Maybe he just needed to hear it from a professional.

Now that she had taken action, Rita calmed down and seemed less determined to fix Richard. She didn't mention finding a counselor. Maybe she clung to the same hope I did—that the mere act of going to a doctor would jolt him into change. Besides, counselors were scarce in the sixties in Natchez, Mississippi.

November 1963

My hands were red and sore from the hot water and detergent as I washed diapers and baby clothes in the kitchen sink. While I scrubbed and rinsed and wrung, I talked to Karen, who was busy in her playpen. The TV was on at a low volume, but the tone of the speaker changed abruptly, attracting my attention. I dried my hands and turned it up. President John Kennedy and Texas Governor John Connolly had been shot in Dallas. It was Friday, November 22.

These first reports were tentative, and I hoped it wasn't so serious after all. I returned to my task briefly, but the gravity of the continuing accounts pulled my attention back to the TV.

I answered the knock on the door in a daze. My parents had been shopping nearby and had also heard early reports of the shooting. They had come on that cold, rainy afternoon to the nearest place where they knew they could follow the coverage.

For a while, we sat riveted to the TV, uttering little more than mumblings of shock and dismay. Karen's cry brought me back to reality. At five months old, she was unaware of the tragedy that had struck our nation. She only knew she was hungry.

As my parents followed the unfolding events, I fed and changed Karen, which reminded me that we grown-ups needed lunch too. The cupboards were nearly bare, but I found a can of tuna, a jar of applesauce, and crackers. No bread. I boiled a couple of eggs and quickly made tuna salad. I shuffled baby things from the table onto the limited counter top, all while trying not to disturb the laundry in progress.

After lunch, I turned my attention back to the laundry; the supply of dry diapers was low. I arranged the wooden clothes rack in front of the open oven door and set the oven temperature to a low setting. The cold and damp of the day made the warmth of the oven welcome.

As the dreary afternoon wore on, long after the death of the president had been confirmed, my parents' attention shifted to my situation. This was the first time they had been in the trailer long enough to witness me juggling tasks in the cramped space, without the benefit of a clothes washer or dryer. I wanted to put it all aside, so as not to evoke their pity, but Karen needed the diapers and clothes.

With the laundry tended to for the moment, I turned to making up more bottles for Karen. I discovered I had only one can of formula, enough to last less than a day. Mother offered to take me to the grocery store. I accepted, hoping she wouldn't notice how little I bought with the few dollars I had. It had been one thing to live in their house and eat their food, but I hadn't actually taken money from them. I felt justified in asking Rita for money because it was her son who failed to provide for me, and also she could more easily afford it.

At the store, Mother's watchful eye didn't miss a thing. "Why aren't you buying more than two cans of formula? That won't last long, will it?"

"Well, it's all I can afford." My cheeks burned. Mother and Daddy exchanged looks.

"You get more formula, and whatever else you need. We'll pay for it," Daddy said. He smiled and winked.

Mother pursed her lips as she nodded her confirmation, the way she did when she felt righteous. I didn't like being the object of anyone's pity, but I especially hated receiving my mother's pity.

While I added to the shopping cart, they talked just out of my earshot.

Back at the trailer, Daddy said, "Bet, I'm going to find a place on the farm to move this trailer, if it's all right with the Walkers. Of course, it'll take time to prepare a site. We'll have to run electricity and dig a well." He gave me a wink and a kiss on the cheek. "I want to have both my girls closer to me."

True to character, the major issue for Mother was image. "It'll be good for you to get out of this trashy trailer park." She was embarrassed that someone might find out where her daughter lived. Moving the trailer to the farm would offer a small improvement.

Daddy's motives were simpler. He simply wanted better conditions for me, and he thought things would be a little better if we were nearer.

Chapter 15
Look at Me

A couple of weeks later, after Friday afternoon had given way to night, dread knotted my gut when I realized Richard should be home. I borrowed Willese's phone to call Rita to see if she knew where he was. She said he and Robert had come in around six and Richard had left for home after a few minutes. He should have been home by six-thirty. The clock read seven thirty-five. Rita offered to come get me, but I declined her invitation to the usual vigil. Karen was cutting teeth; it was easier to comfort her in my own surroundings.

Throughout that night and during the next day, no word came. Richard staggered in the door early Saturday evening, very drunk, and wilder than I had ever seen him. Sneering, he started with his usual accusations. "Looky there at my wife, my perfect little wife. You think you're little miss perfect, don't you?"

"No, I don't think I'm perfect." Even as I said the words, I knew it was no use trying to defend myself.

"You must think you're Jesus H. Christ hisself. Well, you're not. Look at this place. Clothes hanging all over the place. If you were a better wife, I wouldn't stay out and drink so much. What do you say to that?" I'd never heard such scorn in his voice, or seen such hatred in his eyes.

"Why do you always say I think I'm perfect?" I fought to remain calm.

"Because you don't drink, you don't cuss, you don't do anything wrong, do you? You think you're little miss perfect." As the words spewed from his mouth, he pounded his fist on the table.

Karen, who had been playing quietly in the playpen, screamed with fright. Her cry didn't faze him. I picked her up and tried to comfort her. "Please, *please* be quiet. Can't you see you're scaring Karen? You may hate me but I know you love her."

He staggered off to the bedroom. I heard him fumbling with something while I soothed Karen. He returned with his twelve-gauge shotgun and aimed it at me. "I'm gonna put you out of your misery. Just watch and see. But first, I'm going to take you down a peg or two. Take off your clothes."

Richard had never directed such disdain toward me, or threatened me—or anyone else, as far as I knew—with a gun.

I don't know how to react to this.

"What? Why do you want me to take my clothes off?"

"I'm gonna put you on display for the neighbors to see. Take off all your clothes right now, or I'll shoot."

I can't believe this.

"Richard. Please don't make me do this."

"Oh, I'm gonna make you do it all right. Now, get started. Put the baby down and start undressing." He sneered as he wiped the spittle from his mouth.

My body stiffened with fear. I forced myself to breath slowly. I chose my words carefully. "Slow down and think about this. Karen's already scared. I know you love her. If you let me take her next door, I'll come right back and I'll do anything thing you want."

Richard reeled as he thought about it for a moment. "Okay, but if you're not back in two minutes, I'm coming to get you." More drool trickled down his chin and he wobbled before regaining his footing.

Oh, God, please let Willese be at home. She's my only hope.

I rushed out the door with Karen, ran to Willese's, and banged frantically on her door. She opened the door. "What's the matter, honey?" Her eyes opened wide.

"It's Richard. He's drunk and threatening me."

"What can I do?"

"Take Karen for me. And call Richard's mother. Six five four zero four three eight. Please hurry."

Willese called after me, "Be careful," as I dashed back to our trailer.

Richard was slouched against the door when I got back, shotgun still in hand. He again ordered me to undress. This time I had no excuse. I started removing my clothes, first unbuttoning my blouse, as slowly as I could, stalling for time.

As I pretended to get stuck on a button, I thought, *please, Rita, be there, ...and get here quickly. What if she's not at home? Oh, God, please don't let him kill me.*

It's so easy to bargain with God when you're scared for your life.

Richard switched his weight from one leg to the other. "Hurry up and get those clothes off. You're taking too long."

The shoes were off, then the socks. Shaking hands made it difficult enough to unbutton the jeans, but I exaggerated the struggle to get them down over my hips more than necessary, stalling for time.

"Your underwear, too. I want you totally naked." His eyelids drooped and his eyes rolled; he almost drifted off for a moment.

Oh, God, please let him pass out.

No such luck. Richard sucked in a big breath and rallied with renewed energy. "Go ahead. Finish the job."

I slowly removed my bra and then my panties. Sneering with wild-eyed, seemingly perverse pleasure, he moved to the door and opened it wide. He backed away a couple of steps and, directing me with the shotgun barrel, ordered me to stand in the doorway. Humiliation piled on top of fear as I inched to the door.

Please, Dear God, don't let anybody be out there.

I stood a couple of feet inside the trailer. Richard hissed, "No, you can't stop there. I want everybody to get a good look. Go all the way to the door. And yell for everybody to look at you."

He's gone over the deep end.

I closed my eyes and took a deep breath before I moved fully into the doorway.

He said, "Yell for people to look at you."

Keeping my eyes closed, I said, "Look at me."

"Louder," he ordered.

"Look at me," I managed, not much louder. When I peeked between my eyelids, I didn't see anyone.

Thank You, God.

He came up behind me and bellowed, "Hey, everybody. Look at my perfect wife. Get a good look." Peering out, he also discovered no one there. Disappointed, he retreated and told me, "Okay, come back inside. Close the door."

I shook more from fright than from the December cold. I started to put my shirt around my shoulders.

He didn't object. He seemed uncertain about what would come next. His eyelids drooped and his head dipped just for a moment. Then his head suddenly jerked up. He ordered, "Sit in the chair there," pointing to the chair nearest the door.

I wilted into the chair.

He rambled again, with slowed and slurred speech. "You think you're so perfect. And I know you hate me. Well, maybe it's time I put you out of your misery. Maybe I'll just kill us both." He kept the shotgun pointed generally at me, although his aim wobbled. He struggled to keep his eyes open.

"No, Richard, I don't hate you. I love you and I want to help you."

I never did know if he meant to fire the gun or if his finger jerked inadvertently, but the shotgun fired. My eyes closed and I stopped breathing. The sound of the discharge rang in my ears. After a moment, I opened my eyes. Richard looked stunned, too, as if the sound had awakened him from a dream.

I was too stunned to know for sure if I'd been hit. Mentally assessing my body, I realized I didn't feel pain anywhere. Unsure what he would do next, I hesitated to move. The odor of gunpowder permeated the room as a gray smoke rose from the end of the barrel.

After a few moments, I slid my eyes to my left and then to my right. His aim had been off. The blast had shattered the corner of the window and the wall paneling to my left, the closest shot missing me by less than a foot.

I was trying to work out what to do when Rita opened the door. Richard continued to look dumbfounded, his hands relaxing around the shotgun. Frozen in my chair, I was covered with bits of glass, with only my shirt around my shoulders. Muscles here and there twitched involuntarily.

Rita stomped the short distance to Richard, and calmly took the gun. She turned to look me over. "Thank God, you don't look hurt. Are you okay?" She carefully unloaded the gun and put it aside.

"I think so," I whispered.

She flicked the larger pieces of glass off my shoulders, and put my shoes on me so I could get up. "Go put on some warm clothes. I'll take care of him."

By now, I was shaking uncontrollably. I managed to walk to the bedroom, where it was a struggle to get dressed. When I returned, Richard's head hung low and his shoulders sagged as Rita directed him to go sit in her car.

Turning back to me, Rita said, "I'll take him home with me and put him to bed. You get Karen and take care of her. I'll call you tomorrow when he's sobered up."

Though relieved Rita had taken Richard away, I still shook. I rubbed my hands up and down my arms and walked in placed for a couple of minutes in an effort to regain my composure before I went to get Karen.

Willese opened her door slowly this time, not knowing who she would see. When she saw me, she gasped, "Oh, Bettie, thank God it's you. I heard the gunshot and I been aholdin' my breath and prayin' ever since. Are you okay?"

"I'm not hurt, just shaken up. He fired, but he missed me. He got the side of the trailer instead. Do you mind if I sit here for awhile?"

"Course not, honey. I'll make us some hot tea and we'll have a piece of cornbread."

Willese's tea, cornbread, and compassion soothed me. I took Karen home, glad she was sound asleep.

After I settled Karen in her bed, I took another look at the damage from the gunshot. Most of the shot had hit the window, scattering bits of glass over the floor and chair. Only a few shot had landed on the wood paneling. I did my best to clean up the glass. Then I taped a towel over the window to try to keep the cold air out.

Leaden fatigue eventually set in. Sleep came in spurts, and bad dreams woke me abruptly every hour or so.

Rita brought Richard home the next day. She gestured that we should all sit. "Bettie, I waited until we got here to say this because I want you to hear it, too." Turning to him, she straightened her back and set her jaw.

I recognized the look. It was the same look I saw recently when she decided to take Richard to her doctor.

She continued, "Richard, what in heaven's name were you thinking? Did you really intend to kill Bettie? Or my grandbaby? I want some answers." His use of the shotgun was an escalation in behavior that had apparently rattled her; the protective mother had again retreated, replaced by the one determined to repair her broken son.

Richard's shoulders were like rubber. He whimpered, "I don't know, Mom. I only wanted to have a couple of beers with Joel. I guess we had a few more than I intended, and then I don't remember much."

"Don't you know by now you can't drink? Do you remember what Dr. Tischer said?"

He looked down as he shrank further into the sofa. "Yeah, but I just wanted to have one beer with Joel."

Clearly, the visit with the doctor had not helped. When he was sober, he didn't dare resist his mother's tight control, but I sensed that alcohol freed him of those bonds and allowed him to express feelings that he normally held submerged. I started to wonder if that was the primary appeal of drinking for him, if only subconsciously. Apparently, rage was one of his normally submerged feelings. My problem was that the rage had been directed toward me—and at a whole new level.

Rita continued, her voice rising and the color in her face deepening. "Well, do you remember coming home and threatening to kill your wife and your baby? Do you remember shooting out the side of the trailer? Just look at what you did." She waved her hand toward the damaged area.

Richard hung his head and stared at the floor. His face sagged like that of a small boy whose dog just died.

His mother continued, "I've made some calls. It takes two weeks for a full evaluation at the state mental hospital. I want you to go."

My head jerked up.

The state mental hospital? That sounds drastic. But if it will makes him change, then maybe...

Richard hesitated while he processed her words. Speaking softly but deliberately, he said, "Mom. I'm not going to the looney bin. I'm not crazy."

Rita's voice went up a notch. "Well, something's sure wrong with you. Normal people don't threaten their family with a shotgun, or shoot out the side of a trailer."

Over the next hour, Rita's relentless arguments and Richard's own shame combined to wear away his resistance.

"Okay, Mom. I'll do whatever you say. When do I have to go?" He spoke out of complete defeat. He was willing to agree to anything to appease her.

"Next weekend."

"I'll be ready. But I'm not crazy."

Chapter 16

A New Start

January 1964

The state mental hospital in Jackson was a badly neglected facility. Once white, the outside of the building now wore streaked shades of gray and brown, interrupted with the occasional cracked window. Landscaping was dead or overgrown, and weeds had broken through the old asphalt in the parking lot.

Inside, the typical hospital smells assaulted my nose before my eyes adjusted to the surroundings. Two-tone institutional-green walls, darker on the bottom and lighter on top, bore stains, scrape marks, and peeling paint. The glossy black tile floor, worn down from too many steps and too many cleanings, reflected numerous blemishes. The personnel matched the physical appearance of the building, tired and mechanical, as if whatever enthusiasm they had once possessed had faded along with the paint.

In a monotone voice, the intake nurse asked Richard to sign some papers, and then collected all of his personal belongings. A second jaded nurse escorted a frail and frightened Richard down a long corridor. We were unceremoniously given his things, and reminded that no communication was allowed during the two weeks required for evaluation. In spite of everything he had done, all I could feel at that moment was pity.

What would he endure there? I'd heard stories of ghastly treatments performed in mental hospitals and I wondered what diagnostic methods would be used here. I was sure he must be filled with the same questions, although neither of us had spoken about it. Regardless of what fears he harbored, he was powerless in the face of his determined mother. He was, on that day, once again her acquiescent child.

~~~~~~~

Two weeks later, one psychiatrist spoke with Rita while another spoke with me. I didn't know why we had separate conferences, but I was grateful to be included. The psychiatrist who spoke with me reported he had found Richard to be of sound mind, no apparent mental defects.

I responded, "But his behavior isn't normal, is it?"

"No. Certainly not. Richard's lack of control and deep remorse lead me to believe Richard is an alcoholic. Regrettably, we do not treat alcoholism. The most successful program I know of isn't one offered by the medical community. It's the grass roots organization Alcoholics Anonymous. I recommend Richard attend AA meetings."

The doctor also mentioned Al-Anon, a companion organization for family and friends of alcoholics, suggesting I might find support and advice there.

I knew little about alcoholism, or AA. At that time, alcoholism wasn't widely recognized as a disease; most people I knew believed that those who couldn't maintain control over their drinking were common drunks. I didn't know if over-drinking was a disease or not, but I had heard that the AA program was based on a belief in a Higher Power and that seemed like a good start.

Although they had surely been tested, I had steadfastly clung to my basic religious beliefs. I had repeatedly prayed for God to help me, asking only for Richard to stop drinking and wasting money. I had received no recognizable answer, but just because I didn't understand *how* God would answer my prayer didn't shake my faith that He *would* answer my prayer.

I recalled the story in the Gospel of Luke about the woman who appeared repeatedly before a judge, asking for protection from her adversary. The judge didn't grant her request at first, but was finally worn down by her persistence and granted the protection she sought. Perhaps I hadn't prayed long enough, or hard enough, or sincerely enough, or maybe I wasn't asking for the right thing. Nevertheless, I believed God would somehow help me. And I believed God would help Richard, too, if only he would ask. Maybe he would find the answers he needed at AA.

Soon after we were in the car, Richard asked, "Well, what did they say about me? Am I crazy?"

Before I could answer, Rita jumped in, "No, you're not crazy, but you do have a disease. You're an alcoholic. The doctors recommend you go to AA meetings."

Richard bristled. "I'm not a goddamn drunk. I'm not goin' to any meeting with a bunch of drunks. If I decide to stop drinking, I'll do it by myself. I don't need a bunch of drunks preaching to me."

Rita let his response slide. I did too, for the time being, but I harbored hope he would change his mind.

Her next suggestion came as a total surprise. "One more thing. I think you should find another job. I think Joel's a bad influence on you."

By now, I wasn't sure who influenced whom, but I certainly agreed that separating them was better than keeping them together. In addition to the distance from Joel, I also hoped less time with the Walker's would be good for Richard. I wanted him to spend less time within the sphere of their control.

I was astounded when Richard responded, "Yeah… maybe you're right. I think I'll start looking right away."

~~~~~~

Two weeks later, Richard walked in and proudly announced, "Hey, Bet, I've got a new job. I'm gonna be driving a truck for Louisiana Pipe Company in Vidalia. No more crawlin' in tanks way out in the middle of nowhere. How 'bout them apples?" He took one of my hands and put his other hand on my shoulder to twirl me around.

While it was true that truck driving sounded easier than cleaning tank bottoms, I couldn't manage much enthusiasm. My thoughts went immediately to drinking and driving. Still, almost any job away from the Walkers offered at least a little hope. I tried to sound cheerful when I answered, "That's good, honey. Will you be driving local day trips, or will you go cross country?"

"It'll be some of both. They promised the longest I'll be away from home is four days—two days out and two days back. I told 'em I have a wife and baby and I don't want to be gone very long at a time."

Uh-oh. Overnights might provide just too much temptation to drink.

"When do you start?"

"Next Monday. I'll have to be trained for a couple o' days. They'll show me how to fill out the logbook, and some other paperwork, and I'll have to show 'em I can drive those big rigs. There's nothing to it, though, just hauling pipe." Because he had been driving trucks for years, he was confident.

~~~~~~

Richard enjoyed driving. By all indications, he was happier than he had been in quite a while. The separation from Joel and the distance from his parents were exactly what he needed.

He drove for long hours at a time, though. When I asked him if he felt safe about such long stretches, he said, "It's what the company expects from all the drivers. They even showed us how to disconnect the governor, and how to fudge in our logbooks. Fact is, they give us a haul to a certain place, and tell us when we have to be there. If we don't make it on time, we risk getting fired."

"What's a governor?"

"It's a device that limits the speed, so you can't go too fast." Richard admitted the penalties for disconnecting the governor or falsifying a logbook were severe, but insisted that's the way it was done in the trucking business. Or at least that's the way it was done by the company he drove for.

I was skeptical about an established company instructing its drivers on how to skirt the law. But what could I do? I certainly didn't want to tell his parents. His father would be angry, and his mother would probably interfere, maybe even go to the company on his behalf. That's the last thing he needed. And I wasn't about to go to the company myself. I just hoped he didn't get caught—or worse, have an accident.

By March, Daddy had cleared away the brush and weeds in an area about two hundred yards from my parents' house to create a site for the trailer. Easy walking distance but far enough away for privacy. He had gotten an electric power pole installed and a well drilled.

The last task remaining before moving the trailer was to create a driveway by installing a cattle guard over the ditch between the road and the site.

In his eagerness to get the trailer moved, Richard insisted we put a temporary gate in the fence and lay some boards across the ditch, so the mobile home could be moved right away. He promised he would help make a proper cattle guard later. Daddy agreed only because he was eager to get us moved, so he made a makeshift opening in the barbed-wire fence known as a gap. He cut the strands of wire on one side of a fence post, and made wire loops to go over the next post. A gap is usually intended as only a temporary means of opening a fence.

I nervously watched the transport truck creep over the temporary bridge as it pulled the trailer into the pasture. If the bridge didn't hold, I could imagine dishes breaking, doors flinging open, and contents spilling out. But it did hold. With Daddy and Richard supervising, the trailer was settled into its new location. Once it was leveled, the wheels chocked, and the steps put in place, we went inside to inspect for damage. Everything was intact.

We connected power. Nothing sparked, and the lights came on—a good sign. The water supply was connected to the trailer, the pump primed, and we rejoiced when that, too, worked. An inspection of the indoor plumbing revealed no leaks.

Laying the sewage drain was the final step in the plumbing. The proper procedure was to dig a trench at least eighteen inches deep, bury tile pipe, connect the pipe to the drain under the trailer, and cover the drainpipe. Just as he had done about the fence, Richard insisted he need only dig a shallow ditch for now, leading to the nearby drainage ditch. He promised he would bury a proper drain line later. He also said he would put a fence around the new yard to keep the cattle away.

To an outsider, it might appear that the cow pasture outside Ferriday was no better than the trailer park in Natchez, maybe even worse. There was still no clothes washer, no car, and no money. We now parked on the side of the gravel road and came and went through the gap in the fence. Our sewage drained into an open ditch, and cows freely walked up to the windows and rubbed themselves on the side of the trailer. Still, this somehow seemed like an improvement.

Daddy replaced Willese as my closest contact. He stopped in several times a day, more to see Karen than to see me. He usually knelt down to her level and quietly asked, "How's my little ole girl?" The corners of his mouth curled and his bright blue eyes twinkled when he talked to her. She rarely failed to return a beaming smile. He always found it difficult to break away from her baby laughs and squeals of delight at his funny faces and comical noises.

During one of Daddy's visits, after he had played with Karen for a few minutes, a quizzical expression crossed his face as he looked up at me. I knew that look meant he had something on his mind.

My eyebrows went up and the corners of my mouth curled as I waited.

After a few minutes, he said, "Bet, I've been thinking about something. What would you say to having chickens?"

So that was it. Chickens. "I don't know. I've never thought about it. How much work do they require?"

"They're not much trouble. With only a few hens, we'd have a steady supply of fresh eggs. All we need is a chicken coop. The materials won't cost much, and Richard and I can build it. Then we just buy baby chicks, and feed them a couple of times a day. They grow fast. We'd have eggs in no time. How about it?"

He didn't mention anything about wringing chicken's necks and scalding them to loosen their feathers. I had seen that process when I was small and didn't think I'd have the heart for it. I'd prefer to buy my chicken at the store. But a free supply of eggs sounded good. Besides, I was a pushover for most anything Daddy wanted.

"Okay, I'm willing. I'll talk to Richard about it."

Later that evening, when I mentioned it to Richard, he not only agreed, but was excited by the idea. The next day was Saturday and they got together to start on the project.

Like two little boys building their first clubhouse, Daddy and Richard planned, measured, made lists, bought supplies, hammered, stretched wire, and laughed. The coop was finished in only a few days. Then off they went to buy baby chicks and chicken feed. Of course, I knew the job of caring for the chicks would fall to me. But I didn't mind. *What's one more task added to an already long list?*

Just like Daddy said, the chicks grew fast and soon became like pets. Before long, the hens started laying. One decided our front door step was the right place. Each morning, we heard her clucking and clawing, followed by a clink on the metal step. Karen, now a little over a year old, quickly learned to go look for her egg each morning.

Daddy's visits and chickens for pets helped make life in the cow pasture tolerable.

Soon after we got started with the chickens, Richard brought home a discarded, half-working washing machine. The agitator didn't work, but the spin cycle did. Even though it seemed odd to be grateful for something that only half worked, I remembered one of Daddy's sayings: "Be grateful for small favors and large ones in proportion."

The washing machine sat outside in the grass because it was a top-loader and couldn't go under the kitchen counter. I could only go out when Karen was asleep or in a safe place. I tried to limit my time out at the machine to Karen's naps, but since I still had to scrub the clothes by hand, the wash often took longer than her naps. When that happened, I confined her to her playpen to ensure her safety.

I appreciated not having to wring the clothes—the spin cycle still worked fine. But Karen hated being confined to her prison. The woeful sounds of her crying for escape still echo in my head.

~~~~~~

For the first few months after moving the trailer to the farm, Richard's behavior was greatly improved. He had a few nights out, but didn't stay all night and didn't spend as much money as he had in the past. The income from truck driving was a little more than he had made working for his parents, so we usually had enough money to buy the basics.

Most of the time, he was back to that charming fellow who swept me off my feet. He even built a nice sandbox for Karen. About five feet square, it was filled with fine, white sand and outfitted with typical sandbox toys—pail, shovel, and dishes. Daddy, realizing Richard wasn't likely to put up a fence any time soon, kept the cattle out of that pasture most of the time.

We were getting closer to normal every day. I was more hopeful than I had been in a long time that our lives would continue to improve. Deep down, though, I acknowledged that his demons could return at any time.

Therefore, I developed a yearning to save some money so I wouldn't be completely broke the next time Richard failed to make it home with his paycheck.

Life is better here on the farm. If Richard keeps up this good behavior, maybe I can even save enough for a new washing machine.

So far, I had managed to put away only a few dollars, but believed I could save more.

Chapter 17

A Disease?

August 1964

Richard shattered that dream soon enough.

Light, fluffy clouds floated high above Karen and me as we played in the sandbox. Karen poured and stirred sand, making pretend dinner and serving me, her guest. I ate and drank appreciatively.

The ring of the recently-installed telephone jolted me. I left a trail of sand as I scrambled inside to answer it.

It was Richard's mother. He had been in an accident. Out of breath, I gasped, "Is he all right?"

"Yes, he's okay. But it's a miracle. Wait until you see the truck. We took a Polaroid of it."

My spirits fell along with the sand. The accident certainly upset me, but that wasn't the worst part. Richard had phoned her, not me, and she had already been to the accident scene before she called me. Their mother-son bond remained powerful.

Rita's voice interrupted my inner litany of complaints. "There's more."

Of course there is. Let me guess. He was drinking.

"There's a DUI charge pending. As soon as we straighten things out with the police, I'll bring him home."

I slumped against the wall. Rita said the truck had jackknifed. My life had jackknifed along with it. Just when we were making progress, Richard took two steps back. Why did I bother to try? Why did I allow myself to hope? All I ever got in the long run was disappointment.

This is just the way life is. I shouldn't expect things to ever be any different. Why did I allow myself to hope it would be better?

Two hours later, Rita brought Richard home. My jaw dropped when I saw the picture of the truck, which explained why Rita said it was amazing Richard had escaped with nothing more than a few bruises and scrapes. The truck had turned completely over before coming to rest on its side. Studying the picture, I saw every last bit of hope drain out of me just as the gasoline had drained out of the gas tanks in the picture.

Richard had mostly sobered up by this time and, of course, had begun his transition into the apology and contrition phase. I sat off to the side, observing mother and son, too dispirited to say much.

Not Rita. She was irate again.

Straightening her back and raising her chin, she asked Richard, "Do you realize how lucky you are that you aren't lying in a morgue? Or in jail charged with someone's death? We just can't go on like this, wondering when you're going to kill yourself or someone else!"

Richard, as usual, hung his head. His tall frame seemed to be absorbed by the sofa. "I know, Mom. I'm sorry. I promise I'll do better. Just give me another chance."

Rita didn't have a specific plan this time, though. Frustrated, she pointed her finger at Richard and said, "I don't know what we're going to do, but I promise you we're going to do something. I'll talk to you again tomorrow."

I wondered what she would try next. So far, she had suggested counseling, taken him to a doctor, put him in the mental hospital, and tried to get him to go to AA. What was left?

After she stomped out, Richard continued his apology to me, ending with his standard plea for me to help him, except he appeared more sincere than usual. Even so, exactly what he wanted from me remained a mystery.

"Over and over you've asked me to help you, but I don't know what to do. I can't follow you around twenty-four hours a day, can I?"

He slumped down in the sofa even lower, shoulders round and small. "No, I guess not. Maybe there isn't anything you can do, Bet. Maybe Mom's right. There must be something bad wrong with me. I'm just no good, I guess."

He said it more to himself than to me. Darkness and confusion clouded his eyes. I thought I saw demons dancing behind them. His sincerity in that moment caused me to recognize for the first time that he was also miserable and frustrated—I was not the only one in pain.

Fortunately, the DUI charge was dropped. I wasn't sure if it was because of lack of evidence, Richard's glib talk, or because the Walkers bribed another official. I didn't ask any questions. And he didn't get fired. No small miracle. Once again I heard my dad's voice reminding me, "Be grateful for small favors and large ones in proportion."

When Rita returned the next day, she suggested Richard go for ministerial counseling. This met with the same resistance AA had. Richard's sadness and humility had cycled around to defensiveness. "Don't try to tell me I've got the devil in me, cause I don't. I'm not gonna go listen to some preacher tell me I'm a sinner and I'm goin' to hell." He stalked out of the room, refusing to talk about it any further.

Richard's only church experience had been Southern Baptist, and he apparently only remembered the fire and brimstone parts. He didn't mind when I attended my Methodist Church, but he had rarely gone with me. He believed all churches were the same.

Rita had no response to Richard's refusal. She mumbled something about looking for another solution and left. As the days went by, she failed to offer up another plan and dropped the subject.

But her idea set me thinking. My church had a new minister, Jerry—a young, personable, down-to-earth man. I had visited with him a couple of times at my parents'. I remembered him talking about growing up in a dysfunctional family and about counseling alcoholics.

Would Jerry understand someone like Richard?

On a rainy afternoon in June, I left Karen with Daddy and borrowed his car to meet Jerry at the church. He greeted me with his usual ear-to-ear smile and a bear hug. Jerry was a robust man, kind of pear-shaped. He kept his dark, thick hair in a crew cut, and wore black-rimmed glasses. He preferred white, short sleeve shirts year-round, always with a tie. But even if he had put a pocket-protector in his pocket and tape on his glasses, his joviality would never have allowed him to be mistaken for a nerd. Bubbling with cheerfulness, he settled behind his desk and asked, "What brings you here on this fine day?"

"Fine day? It's cloudy and raining."

"Every day is fine. We need rain as much as we need sun."

I started out a little skeptical of someone so optimistic. "I want to talk about my husband, Richard. I think he has a drinking problem."

"Tell me about him."

"His behavior cycles. Most of the time, he's kind, works hard, and tries to be responsible. But every so often, something inside him snaps and he goes on a drinking binge. He convinces himself he can have one beer. One leads to two, and then he doesn't stop. Sometimes he's out only one night, but other times he's gone for a weekend or longer. And he usually spends all the money he has with him."

Jerry nodded. "Sounds familiar. Do you know much about alcoholism?"

"No, I guess not. Is it an allergy to alcohol?" The psychiatrist at the state mental hospital had said he believed Richard was an alcoholic, but hadn't elaborated on the disease or its treatment. His only suggestion had been AA, which Richard had refused to consider.

"Some people think it's a physiological disorder, and others think it's mental. Either way, the symptoms are the same, and the ways of dealing with it are the same."

"Tell me more."

"It's one of the most destructive diseases in our society, and yet few people understand it. Many still regard the alcoholic as a common drunk."

"What's the difference?"

"Alcoholism affects people in different ways. Some alcoholics drink only in the evening, others drink throughout the day, every day. Many learn to function well enough that most people don't realize they're drinking. Still others are binge drinkers. Usually, they're the ones who lose all control when they're drinking. It sounds like Richard falls into that category."

"How do you know if a person is an alcoholic or not?"

"Oh, there's a checklist of eight or ten questions, but the most important one has to do with control. Does he control his drinking, or does the drinking control him? Many people drink by choice, and even if they drink a lot, they can stop if they want.

"They decide how much they want to drink and have no problem sticking with the plan. They might even start out to get drunk, and they do. But if they want to have only a couple of drinks, they're able to stop there."

I shook my head. "That doesn't sound like Richard."

"For the alcoholic, the alcohol has control. He's unable to stick by his limits—he becomes powerless to resist. From what you say about Richard, he sincerely wants to stop or control his drinking, but he can't. That's the difference."

That's it. Control. Jerry's definition certainly fits Richard. If he's an alcoholic, that's a lot better than being crazy, or simply a mean drunk.

I nodded. "Yeah, I think he does want to stop. After a binge, when he's apologetic, it seems as if he's hurting as much as I am. He seems truly sorry, and appears to genuinely want to be different. But after a day or so, his attitude starts to change; he gradually becomes more confident and then defensive. Sometimes I can predict when he's about to go on a binge just by his attitude. When he gets cocky, I get scared."

"That's sounds typical. He probably hates the part of himself that can't control his drinking, so he justifies himself.

Eventually, he needs to prove to himself he can have one drink like other people. Of course, when he starts, he can't stop."

"What can I do to help him, Jerry?"

"I'm sorry to say that's an age-old question with no easy answer. Has he been to AA? That's the most helpful program I know about."

"No, he won't hear of it. He declares he's no drunk and he doesn't need to be with a bunch of drunks."

"Too bad, but not surprising. In truth, there's not much anyone else can do for him until he admits he has a problem. I know that's not what you want to hear."

"No, it's not. I just want a decent life for us, and for Richard to not be abusive, or spend too much money. Is that selfish?"

"No, not at all. So now the question is how can I help you?"

"You already have. You've helped me understand his condition better. I wish I could get Richard to come and talk to you. If he could understand he has a disease, maybe he'd be willing to get help."

Jerry grinned. "Maybe we can work on that. We know confronting him directly won't work, but what if I simply drop by for a visit occasionally? After all, a minister needs to call on his flock, doesn't he?" Jerry winked. "And if, while I'm there, I happen to start talking about my father's drinking, or someone else I've known, well..."

"Sounds good, Jerry. I'll make plenty of tea." He smiled. Jerry had quite a reputation for drinking large quantities of iced tea.

Jerry prayed with me before we ended the visit. I left Jerry's office feeling more hopeful than I had in a long time.

Please, God, give Jerry the right words to reach Richard. And open Richard's ears and heart to hear them.

During Jerry's first visit, Richard's grin told me he liked Jerry. He confirmed this after Jerry left. "You know, he's all right for a preacher. I kind of like him."

Hmm. This is a promising start.

Jerry proceeded slowly and cautiously, getting to know Richard and showing he wasn't all about "fire and brimstone." If Richard realized the coincidence that he was at home each time Jerry came to visit, he never let on, and he clearly enjoyed Jerry's visits. Jerry carefully avoided the word alcoholic, but he described people under the grip of drinking, and told stories of people who lost control when they drank. He also included a few personal stories from having grown up with a father who drank too much.

I hoped Richard would see himself in some of those stories.

Richard didn't come right out and admit he had a drinking problem, but he looked thoughtful each time he heard another of Jerry's tales.

~~~~~~

Things were still hard. No cattle guard had been installed, no proper sewage line had been installed, no fence had been installed around the trailer, and I still installed myself in the yard to do laundry. But certain aspects of our lives were far more important than those. Richard was making decent money and managing to get most of it home. He enjoyed the visits with Jerry, and hadn't gone on a binge in weeks.

Hope surfaced once more. This time, with Jerry's influence, Richard was becoming a responsible husband and father.

We are going to be all right after all.

Chapter 18

New Job, New Hope

September 1964

At last we were a regular family, even if we were struggling. The improvement fueled my belief that I could continue to will things to happen according to my plan. And my plan did not include having an only child. The time had come to have another baby.

Richard had just come in from helping Daddy repair fence, one of the never-ending tasks on the farm. He sat on the floor playing with Karen. "Look at her, Trinkatunia. She's running to me." He swooped her up in his arms and they both giggled. Karen had been walking for only a month, so we were still growing accustomed to seeing her walk and run.

"Richard, what do you think about having another baby? We've always said we don't want an only child."

"Well, Karen's walking and she's talking more every day. Since she's Daddy's girl, I guess we do need to have a baby for you. I expect we need to have a little brother for Karen."

"You don't think it's too soon, do you?"

"Not if you don't. You have the hard part. If you get pregnant as quickly as you did the first time, they'd be about two years apart. Don't you think that's about right?"

"Yes, that's the spacing I've always wanted."

"Let's go for it then."

A little more than six weeks later, Dr. Gibson confirmed I was pregnant. We waited a few more weeks before we told our families. All four grandparents issued the standard congratulations, but they couldn't conceal their concern. I pretended not to notice.

They'll see. This pregnancy will go well, and our little family will be happy. Richard's grown up now. Everything will be fine. They'll see.

Morning sickness was milder and shorter—another sign my willpower was working. Our lives were almost normal, except that we still lived in a cow pasture. Most of the time I forgot my isolation—until something forced me to remember.

Soon after Becky and Stan joined our church, Becky joined the choir. We seemed to be drawn to each other. We were near the same age, and she had a baby boy about the same age as Karen.

One Sunday she invited me to visit her. Her home was modest, but nicely furnished. We enjoyed chatting and watching our babies play. I enjoyed the afternoon, feeling almost normal. But after I left, I realized I couldn't possibly reciprocate. My pride couldn't bear the thought that she would see where I lived. And I couldn't continue to accept her invitations *without* reciprocating. When she invited me over again, I made up an excuse. She soon stopped asking. I never told her the real reason.

Richard slipped up a couple of times soon after we learned I was pregnant, but he stayed out only one night and didn't spend all his money. Those brief incidents were easily forgiven and quickly forgotten.

In mid-December, Richard looked up from the paper. "Hey, Bet. Listen to this. Here's a job working for a barge line on the Mississippi River." He had grown tired of driving a truck and had been watching the ads for a few weeks.

"Working on the river, huh? What's the job?"

"It's for a deckhand. I know I'd be starting at bottom, but it would be better than driving a truck. I'm gonna call." He reached for the phone and dialed. He smiled as he hung up. "I have an interview tomorrow at ten."

~~~~~~

"Guess what? I got the job." Richard's face looked like a child's on Christmas morning. "I'll be working on the Mississippi from north of St. Louis to New Orleans, stopping at each major town. I'll start out as a deckhand, but I can move up if I work hard. I'll be gone from two to six weeks each trip, and then have one day off for every two worked. So I could have from one to three weeks off at a time. And the pay's a good bit better than I'm making now."

"You're excited about this, aren't you?"

"Yeah, I am. I think I'm gonna like this." His face softened, as did his voice. "And, Bet, the best part is I can't drink while I'm on the river."

After his many conversations with Jerry, he had finally admitted, at least some of the time, that he needed to limit his drinking. He didn't go so far as to say he shouldn't drink at all, but this shift in thinking marked a major milestone. That he thought of the job as a way of controlling his behavior sounded good, but I wanted to be sure I understood. "There isn't any alcohol on the barges or tows?"

"Nope, it's not allowed. Strict rules."

"That's good." My thoughts turned next to the long periods of time away from work. Could he maintain sobriety with days of free time and no structure?

Richard continued, "And one more thing. My checks will be mailed here to you, so you'll have control of the money." He raised his eyebrows and smiled, as if to ask, "What could be better than that?"

An increase in salary, and I would get the checks. I had to admit it sounded nice. "Sounds pretty good. When do you start?"

"The first week in January, right after Christmas."

January, 1965

At the train station in Brookhaven, Mississippi, Richard hugged Karen goodbye, and held me close. But Richard-the-Tom-Sawyer-adventurer was eager to begin his exploration of the mighty Mississippi. Even though we shared emotional goodbyes, he was eater to get going when he set off to Alton, Illinois, to catch the boat.

He seemed to welcome a restricting yet exciting work environment, and was confident he could stay sober on his days off. If only I'd help him. Once more, I wondered how to do that.

~~~~~

"How did it go?" I asked two weeks later, greeting him as he got off the boat in Natchez.

Richard's infectious smile radiated satisfaction as he gathered Karen up into his arms, "It was great. I learned so much, Bet. I can't wait to go back—after I've had some time with my girls." He had Karen giggling already. He hugged me with his free arm.

As we drove home, I asked, "What are your plans for your time off?"

"Oh, I figure you can use a little help around the house, and I can give your dad a hand, too." I believed he was sincere, but I also knew it would take no small miracle for him to stay close to home and survive the week without a drinking binge.

Never much good at domestic duties other than cooking, his contribution at home consisted mainly of playing with Karen, checking on the chickens, and helping Daddy with some fence and barn repairs. The time flew by until only two days remained, Richard sober and me with my fingers crossed. Could he make it? Two days later, we said goodbye at the Natchez dock as he happily embarked on another tour of duty.

He had made it! Maybe this job was a magic elixir after all.

~~~~~~

Three days after Richard left, a particularly harsh cold snap descended on us. As the outside temperature dropped, so did the inside temperature. I checked the thermostat—it was still set at seventy-two—but the thermometer read sixty-five. I toggled the switch and listened. No sound from the heater. No warm air flowing. We were out of butane. A tank mounted on the front of the trailer supplied butane to the heater, the gas stove, and the water heater. I had asked Richard to check the level before he left, and he assured me we had plenty.

I wonder if he really checked it, or if he just misjudged. Why haven't I learned to do this myself?

Regardless, the tank was empty and I didn't have the money to have it filled. Richard's first check wouldn't arrive for another week. I was broke.

I called Rita and asked her if she would buy butane for me and allow me to repay her when I received Richard's check. She readily agreed, but she couldn't bring it to us until the next day. Meanwhile, the temperature in the thin-walled trailer was falling rapidly. The inside thermometer now read fifty-eight. The temperature outside was in the mid-thirties and predicted to dip into the teens that night. How could I keep us warm until the next day?

Mother was still working nights and sleeping during the day, so I couldn't go there. We had a small electric heater we used for heating the bathroom while we bathed Karen. I moved it into my bedroom at the end of the trailer. As in most single-wide mobile homes, the bed took up most of floor space in the room. I piled toys, books, diapers, snacks—and Karen—onto the bed. I was grateful she was such a calm child for nineteen months old, and so easy to entertain.

Richard had broken the room's pocket door during one of his outbursts, and with nothing blocking the airflow in and out of the room, the small heater made little difference. I needed a way to block the doorway. I folded an old sheet into thirds and used small nails to fasten it to the wall over the doorway to restrict airflow. The room was still cold, but considerably warmer than the rest of the trailer. We stayed under covers as much as possible. Karen didn't seem to mind; she had my undivided attention as I entertained her.

Forced to camp in one room, struggling to keep warm, I settled into depression and self-pity. Perhaps it was made worse because I had been so hopeful lately. Then I remembered the old saying "It gets darkest just before the dawn." We stood on the threshold of a better life. Richard had just proven he could handle the time off. I tried to buck up.

We survived the night, and daylight brought renewed hope. If we could only make it a few more hours...

Rita arrived shortly before noon with the butane. First, I splurged by setting the thermostat to seventy-five to get the trailer thoroughly warm. Then as soon as the water had time to heat, I drew a hot bath. I put Karen in with me, and we played in bubble bath until we were both thoroughly warm. Able to cook again, I then made us a hearty meal. The warmth buoyed my spirits and my optimism returned.

Chapter 19

Go Have My Baby

The job for the barge company suited Richard. He always had stories to tell when he came home. I don't remember the hierarchy of jobs on a barge, but he had already moved up one rung on the ladder. In fact, he liked the environment so much that he spoke of eventually getting his pilot's license.

For the next few months, he handled the time off the boat well, too. We were not quite normal—we still lived in a cow pasture and I still used a half-working washing machine—but we were not as dysfunctional as we had been the year before. We had fun watching Karen grow and learn, and we all eagerly anticipated the new baby.

June 1965

Dr. Gibson had calculated my due date to be June thirteenth, Karen's birthday. While I knew the odds of actually delivering on that day were slim, I secretly hoped I would. Richard left on the eighth as planned, but the company had agreed to let him off the boat immediately if I called.

We needn't have worried. The thirteenth came and went, and the eighteenth, and the twenty-third...

He returned home as scheduled on the twenty-fifth to find me no closer to delivering than when he had left on the eighth.

Sunday morning, the twenty-seventh, Richard asked, "How do you feel, Bet?"

"I feel okay, just tired of waiting. Why?"

"I was thinking about going fishing. You think you'd be able to go?"

I thought for a minute. We hadn't been fishing in a long time and we both enjoyed fly-fishing. Rita and Ed had come the evening before to take Karen home with them until after the baby came. We all knew I couldn't go much longer. Since we were alone, this was a good opportunity for us to go fishing, and I was flattered he wanted me to go with him.

"I'd like to go, but do you think I can get into the boat safely?"

Richard grinned. "I'll help you into the boat, and take good care of you, don't worry. I know a place it'll be easy."

I couldn't resist. We packed a lunch and gathered the fishing gear.

By noon, a full two weeks past my due date, we parked at one of the myriad bodies of water along the Mississippi called Old River—pockets of water left behind on the lower Louisiana side of the Mississippi River when the river had changed course. Known for good fishing, those lakes were one of the reasons Louisiana is known as Sportsman's Paradise. Typically, this one was long, narrow, and winding, and lined with cypress trees draped with scarves of Spanish moss swaying in the gentle breeze.

Richard held the small, wooden boat firmly against the dock as he helped me into it. Then he loaded the fishing gear, cooler, and food. He slowly paddled along the shore while we fly fished. The warm sun and pleasant breeze combined to make the kind of day that makes the skin tingle and eases the mind. I didn't really care if we caught fish or not.

Richard cautioned me, "Now if you need anything, or notice anything unusual, you tell me and we'll go back. I don't want to be delivering a baby out here on the lake."

Few other people were out and the fish were biting. We caught medium-sized bream, six to eight inches long. After a few hours, we had filled the creel. But about that time we made an unfortunate discovery. I was sunburned. I had forgotten to cover my fair skin. Once we noticed my redness, we knew I must get to shade immediately.

Back at home, Richard made a baking soda paste—the best remedy we knew—and bathed me with it before cleaning the fish. He cooked some and put the rest in the freezer.

By Monday morning, the redness and pain of my sunburn had lessened, and I was having light contractions. At last!

~~~~~~

Dr. Gibson's first words were, "What in the world were you doing to get such a sunburn?"

"Fishing."

"Fishing? Where?"

"On Old River."

He laughed. "Two weeks overdue and you were in a boat fishing? I wish I could have been there! Oh, well, except for the sunburn, it seems to have done you no harm. You're not in labor yet. You're only having Braxton-Hicks contractions. Go back home and call me if anything changes. But if nothing happens by Thursday, I might induce you."

By noon, Richard had me and my contractions back home. He said, "Now that you're back here, and not actually in labor, do you mind if I go fishing again? The fish were biting so well yesterday, I want to go back for enough to fill the freezer. I promise I'll be back before dark."

If he hadn't been so sweet lately, I might have worried, but my confidence was sky-high. Besides, I welcomed having some time alone. I knew I wouldn't rest again for a long time after the baby came.

I read for a while, napped, and woke up a little before dusk. *Richard should be home soon, so I'll start dinner.*

Eight o'clock came and no Richard. By nine o'clock, I knew he was no longer fishing, and only one explanation seemed plausible. The familiar pain of dashed hopes and betrayal rose up and encircled my heart.

Why does he have to go and mess it all up just when he was being so sweet?

Eventually I slept, but woke several times with bad dreams. Tuesday morning, I felt light contractions, but they were neither regular nor strong.

Richard staggered in about three o'clock Tuesday afternoon, drunk and still drinking. He held two six-packs of beer, one partially gone. "Well, hey there, Trinkatunia. How are you this fine day?" When he was drinking, the nickname sounded like a slur.

"I'm fine."

With bleary eyes and an unsteady stance, he said, "Well, I'm fine, too! The fish weren't biting, so I decided to have myself a beer—or two or three." His grin widened into a repulsive sneer.

He puttered with fishing gear for a few minutes before his mood abruptly changed to anger and resentment. "Why haven't you had that baby yet anyway? What's the matter with you?"

"I don't know, Richard."

"Well, I think it's time we get it over with."

"What do you mean?"

"We'll take you up to that hospital so you can have my baby boy."

"That's okay. If I need to go to the hospital, I'll call Daddy to take me."

"Oh, no, you won't. You think I'm not capable of taking my own wife to the hospital? Get your stuff and come on with me." He started toward me.

I backed away as he attempted to grab my arm. He stumbled and fell against me, knocking me down with him. As we both struggled to our feet, I saw the hostility in his eyes. It had been a long time since I'd seen that look, but the memory of it frightened me. I decided I'd rather risk a car accident than a fight. A quick inventory of my body told me I was as yet unharmed. I grabbed my purse and hospital bag that were already near the door.

"Come on with me," he said again, this time successfully grabbing my arm. "We're gonna have us a baby." He jerked me out the door and to the car, and shoved me in. Tires squealed as we started out, and the car skidded several times. Amazingly, we made it through town and to the hospital without an accident.

Richard swerved into the front drive of the hospital and screeched to a stop. I was shaken, but grateful we had made it intact, especially since he had finished another beer on the way. Even though it took some effort, he managed to get out of the car and around to my side before I could get away from him. He caught up with me and grabbed my arm, holding it tightly, using it to steer me to the front door of the hospital. He opened the door, pushed me inside and spewed, with drool hanging from his mouth and loud enough for all to hear, "Now go have me a baby." He stumbled back outside and headed for the car.

When he pushed me inside, I bumped into a chair in the waiting area, half falling. I braced myself against the chair, keeping my gaze down. I didn't want to see who was watching. I felt heat rise in my cheeks as I fought to hold back tears. Out of nowhere, I felt a comforting arm around my shoulder and a kind voice saying, "Come with me, sweetie. I'll take care of you."

I turned to see a smiling nurse. She gently guided me out of the waiting area and down a hall.

I whispered, "Can you tell Elizabeth Wailes I'm here? She's my mother."

"Sure, honey. I'll find her right away."

Before long, I was installed in a private room, Mother with me. If possible, Mother was even more embarrassed about Richard's behavior than I was. Word of "that awful man who pushed his pregnant wife in the front door" had traveled throughout the hospital. We heard people passing my door whispering about it. Mother advised me to ignore everyone else and to think only about myself and the baby. I decided she probably felt enough anxiety and embarrassment for both of us, so I relaxed a little. At least I was safely away from Richard.

Contractions came and went throughout the evening, but with no increase in intensity. A little past eleven, we were awakened by Richard bursting through the door of my room, with two nurses trailing behind, saying insistently, "You can't go in there. You're not allowed in this area this late at night. Sir, you'll have to go."

He ignored them, and barged into the center of the room and glowered down at me. Unstable and slurring his words, he said, "Well, just look at you, Little Miss Priss. You think you're perfect, don't you? You think you're Jesus H. Christ hisself. If you're so perfect, why haven't you had that baby yet?"

When I didn't answer, he spun around to glare at Mother. She feigned sleep, but that didn't stop him from saying, "And that goes for you, too, 'Lizbeth." With those words, he spat in her face, turned on his heel, and headed for the exit.

The nurses went in search of help, but they were too late. Richard's long legs took him back out just as quickly as he had come in.

Moments later, a nurse returned to tell us they had alerted the police and promised he wouldn't get into the hospital again.

An hour later, a light tap on my door awakened me. A police officer quietly entered to tell me Richard was in jail, having been arrested for trying to steal a watermelon from a convenience store not far away. A charge of disturbing the peace had been added, too. Richard would be held for at least a week.

Chapter 20
Coming Home

By midday Wednesday, the contractions were still light and only eight to ten minutes apart, so Dr. Gibson ordered a Pitocin drip to induce labor. Contractions intensified and I soon transitioned into hard labor. Mother accompanied me to a labor room around five, and before long, to the delivery room. At six forty-five, I was overjoyed to hear, "It's another girl."

Even though everyone else in the family wanted a boy, I had secretly hoped for another girl. I thought two girls would be better friends to each other than a boy and girl. The prospect of raising two girls seemed easier, too, with the possibility lurking in the back of my mind that I would likely be raising them with little help. Confidence that I could "will" my life to turn out according to my plan had evaporated once again.

Richard had been so sure of a boy he had refused to even discuss girls' names. With him now absent, I gave her the name I wanted—Linda Katherine.

Dr. Gibson kept me in the hospital beyond the standard three-day stay. He wanted me fully rested and recovered when I went home to face the inevitable stress that awaited me. The extra time gave me the chance to think about my future.

Here in the hospital, I'm safe and protected, but what about when I go home? And I do have to go home. There is no place else. No job experience, no job qualifications, no car, no child care, no place to live. The Walkers wouldn't allow me to stay in the trailer without Richard, even if I could persuade him to move out.

And I'm so embarrassed. Before now, Richard did his drinking and misbehaving mostly in Natchez and Vidalia, but this time Richard showed his bad side in my territory. News travels fast in a small town, and anyone in Ferriday with ears has probably heard what happened. I dread even going to the grocery store.

The nurses seemed to give me extra attention, as much out of respect for Mother as sympathy for me. One of the people who pampered me was the director of nurses. On the day I left, she came to visit one last time. She sat on the side of my bed and took my hand. "You know, if you want a job, I'll hire you as a nurse's aid. I can't promise you great pay, but I'll waive the requirement for the six-week training course and give you personal, on-the-job training. You probably already know half of it from your mother anyway. You can start at full salary, a hundred seventy-five a month."

Even in a small town in 1965, this wouldn't cover rent, car payment, childcare, and food. As much as I appreciated the offer, I had to decline.

~~~~~~

Linda was six days old when Mother brought us home from the hospital. Mother was still helping me get settled when Rita drove up with Karen and Richard. Karen had been with Rita since the day before the fishing trip. During the week and a half, I had only seen her the two times Rita brought her to the hospital to see her new baby sister, so I was overjoyed to have her back at home.

Seeing Richard again was a different story. We exchanged strained, awkward looks, each wondering what to say. It was hard to tell if Richard was more embarrassed at seeing Mother or me. He avoided eye contact with both of us, and looked as if he'd rather explode than talk to either of us. Even Rita, usually so strong and confident, looked uneasy.

Karen, excited to see her sister in person, broke the tension. "Can I hold my new baby?"

All four of us adults immediately focused our attention on her, relieved she provided a neutral focal point so we didn't have to speak directly to each other. We put Linda in her lap for a few minutes. Karen smiled and Linda, and petted her tenderly, and said, "Hello, baby."

After just a couple of minutes, Karen began to squirm, so Richard reached for Linda. He also pulled Karen up into his lap.

Mother and Rita stood apart and looked uncomfortable. Even without the events of the previous week, there wouldn't have been much warmth between them—there never had been. Their backgrounds and personalities couldn't have been more different. Mother soon excused herself, and Rita followed a short time later.

Finally alone, Richard looked at me with questioning eyes. Perhaps he sensed a new coolness from me, or perhaps he didn't know where to begin, or maybe he thought his week in jail had been punishment enough. Regardless, he didn't bother with his usual apologies and contrition. He was scheduled to leave in a few days, anyway, so he simply avoided talking of the recent events, and focused his attention on the girls.

~~~~~~

After Richard left for a six-week stint on the boat, I devoted my time and attention to my two girls, happy to have him out of my way. Karen eagerly took on the role of big sister, and the three of us soon settled into a comfortable routine.

By the time Richard returned, my desire to escape had faded. I had once again grown accustomed to my little nest, even with its difficulties. I chose the path of least resistance and ignored the issue.

Until Richard forced me to face it again.

Chapter 21

The Daydream

August 1965

On his second day off the boat, Richard went out for groceries. After a couple of hours had passed, I knew not to expect him home that night. I called his mother to report him missing. This time she searched by herself, after which she came over to report she hadn't found him. She stayed with me the remainder of the night and into the next day.

When there was still no word by the afternoon, Rita went home. She called the next day. "Who do you suppose he could be with?"

"Only one person I can think of." We both said, "Joel" at the same time.

Rita called Joel's house and, sure enough, he had gone missing, too. Certain they were together, we could do nothing but wait until their money ran out and they needed to be rescued.

Three days later, Rita called to say, "They're in Little Rock, Arkansas, or at least they were there two days ago. My bank just called. Richard wrote a bad check to a Ford dealership in Little Rock."

How could he have written a check? He doesn't even have a checking account. And why to a Ford dealership? Richard has a Chevrolet truck.

Recently, I had closed our joint account and opened one in my name only. I had gotten tired of having my checks bounce because of Richard. He would write a check and not tell me. Thinking I knew our balance, I would write a check, only to have it not paid because of insufficient funds.

"How much is the check for? What did he have done to the truck?"

"Oh, he didn't have work done," Rita said. "He traded it in on a new truck. He wrote a check for $2,194.68—payment in full for a new truck. He used an old check from your joint account."

"And the dealer took it? Don't they verify checks that large? If they'd called the bank, they would have found out that account's closed."

"That's not all. If he had simply overdrawn an open account, it wouldn't be so bad. But my bank explained that writing a check with no account is a federal offense. Of course, I'm going down to the bank and cover the check so the bank won't notify the dealer. I can't allow him to get arrested on a federal check-writing charge."

I couldn't believe he could walk into a dealership more than two hundred fifty miles from home, in another state, trade in his old, beat-up truck, and walk out with a new one, paid for with an unverified personal check. Even though the dealer was stupid, that didn't excuse Richard.

If it was up to me, I'd let him get arrested and prosecuted. He should pay for his crime. But Rita will never let that happen.

Rita called again a little later. "I covered the check. And I called the dealer to get a lead on where he is. He gave a local address that I believe is a relative of Joel's. I'm sending Robert to get them. I don't want them to leave there, drunk, in a brand new truck I've just paid for. Will you go with Robert?"

Richard's younger brother Robert didn't want to drive that far alone; he was only eighteen. I didn't want to leave the girls, especially Linda. I hadn't been successful in nursing Karen. With Linda, though, nursing was going very smoothly. But I knew Richard's family would make me feel guilty if I said no. Under pressure to decide quickly, I caved in. "Yes, I'll go. When do we leave?"

"We'll be over within the hour. Get the girls ready, and I'll bring them back with me."

Robert and I drove all night. We found Richard and Joel the next day at the address Rita had given us. Of course, after this much time, I had missed several feeding times, and my breasts were about to explode.

On the way home, as his head cleared, Richard started in. "Bet, I'm so sorry. I'll make it up to you. I promise. This time I mean it. I'm gonna straighten up and fly right. You'll see. If only you'll help me, I know I can do better." He reached for my hand.

Which I withdrew quickly. "Do you know how many times I've heard the same promises? I'm tired of hearing it, Richard. I don't want words, I want action. If you really mean it, do something to show me you're serious."

"What do you want me to do?"

"You can grow up and be responsible. You've got two children now, or have you forgotten that? You can stay away from Joel, or anyone else you drink with. You can go to work, and not squander your pay. And you can admit that you simply cannot drink. Nothing at all."

"I will, Trinkatunia I promise."

I wanted to believe him. I wanted my love for him to wash away this latest incident like it had washed away all those before, but the wellspring of love and forgiveness that had flowed so freely from my heart for so long had now slowed to a trickle.

So had my breast milk.

Because I had been away for a day and a half, my milk production had almost stopped and Linda had gotten used to a bottle. The combination of missed feedings and stress resulted in me being unable to resume breastfeeding. As if there weren't already enough reasons to be angry about Richard's latest stunt, the breastfeeding issue was especially emotional for me—one I would resent for many years.

~~~~~

During the next few months, each day seemed to be a more difficult struggle than the day before. Living in the trailer in a cow pasture, still doing laundry partially by hand in the yard wore me down physically and emotionally.

This time I couldn't simply forgive Richard and move forward. His escapade at the hospital had affected me more deeply than any of his earlier stunts. And I kept thinking about the job offer—a hundred seventy-five dollars a month. Not nearly enough for me to live on. The hard fact remained that there were no jobs in the area for which I qualified that paid any more, certainly not enough to support two babies and me.

Day after day of despair plunged me into a deep abyss of hopelessness. I continued to search for some way to escape, but I felt trapped just as surely as an animal in a cage. There was simply no way out.

I made every effort to stay in control on the surface, but underneath my emotions roiled. My increasing tension affected my babies, too. Linda, probably sensing my emotional distance, demanded my undivided attention, clinging to me for hours at a time. She often had little appetite and didn't gain weight like most babies. Even at nine months old, she was thin. When she refused to eat, or fussed when I put her down, I had little patience and often screamed at her, which only exacerbated the situation.

Karen wasn't spared from my anxiety. I demanded much more of her than was reasonable for a child as young as she was. I had her care for Linda far too often, and I required her to help with chores such as folding laundry and cleaning her room.

In short, I had become a shrew.

I retreated further into isolation from anyone other than immediate family and tried to keep my concerns to myself. I didn't discuss my disquiet with my parents because I didn't want to increase their worry. I also didn't want their pity and—most importantly—I didn't want them to think I was asking for help. I firmly believed I was the one who had gotten myself into such a sorry state, and it surely wasn't my parents' responsibility to help me out of it.

My relationship with Ed had always been distant, and I already knew Rita's point of view was warped, so I didn't voice my concerns with either of them.

I was not only mired in hopelessness and self-pity, but the loneliness had become acute.

This is when I started having the daydream.

At unexpected moments, perhaps while cooking, or folding the laundry, this same scene played out in my mind. In it, I dropped what I was doing, ran out the door and into the road. I shucked clothes along the way until I was totally naked and babbling incoherently. I held my hands over my ears to shut out even my own voice. I saw myself running into the distance, away from everything familiar, and especially away from everything in my current life. As my image grew smaller, faceless people in white coats magically appeared and gently lifted me away to some other realm. In that peaceful place, I was cared for by compassionate people. No more worries or responsibilities.

Off to the side of the scene, equally nice people scooped up my children and transported them to the same blissful place where they, too, were well cared-for and happy.

This magical place was a dreamy utopia, a place I was welcome to stay as long as I liked. No more cares or worries.

Each time I had this vision, when the illusion of escape was at its most delicious, an interruption brutally snatched me back to reality.

After slipping into this daydream multiple times, I began to worry.

Am I losing my mind? These aren't the thoughts of a normal person. I need help. But from whom?

I couldn't bear to confess these thoughts to my parents or to the Walkers. I had no friends. Even if I knew someone to talk with, I had no car and no one to watch the kids.

Only one person would come to me, wouldn't think I was crazy, and would try to understand. Maybe he could help me regain my sanity.

Jerry Means, our minister.

He was the only person outside of my family who had been to the trailer. He hadn't visited for some time, though, not since Richard had lost interest in talking to him.

But I trusted him. It was time to call Jerry again—this time for me.

～～～～

On the tattered old sofa with a tall glass of iced tea, Jerry listened to my accounts of Richard's recent behavior. I explained that I felt helpless. I explained that my despair had deepened and I explained the recurring daydream.

"Am I crazy?"

"No, you aren't crazy. Your mind is simply seeking a brief escape from your anxiety."

"That's just it. I would like to escape, but I feel powerless to change anything about my life. I can't leave Richard because I can't support myself. I will not go back to my parents or to Richard's parent. And I just don't think anything will ever change."

Jerry spoke quietly. "You aren't powerless. You just haven't discovered your power yet. But you will. Keep praying about it."

Throughout the course of the continuing discussion, I began to see that, until then, I had yielded to the forces of those around me, just as the will-of-the-wisp bends to the direction of the wind.

Jerry leaned forward. "You don't always have to be the one to *react*, Bettie. You can be the one to *act*. Most of what we perceive as limits are actually self-imposed. Sometimes, when we think about it, we can move those limits. If we want change badly enough, we find a way to move past those old limits, and we discover new possibilities."

～～～～

Little by little, the perception of my world changed. As if a fog slowly lifted, I stopped believing Richard's drinking was my fault. As that happened, my despair gradually turned into anger. Or maybe

I just recognized the deep, seething anger I had suppressed for so long.

I talked with Jerry again.

"Jerry, lately I'm not so much depressed as I am angry. I'm angry that my life has turned out like this. I'm angry at Richard for not providing better for us. I'm angry at his mother for making him the way he is. I'm even angry at myself for my poor choices. I'm just angry at life. I need help getting past all this rage."

"I agree you will be happier with less anger, but anger isn't necessarily all bad. It's all right to be angry with those things that are bad for us. Sometimes it's even good. It's what we do with the anger that makes the difference. Anger can be a wonderful motivator. If you channel it in the right way, anger can become determination, and then determination can become action."

~~~~~~

During the next few weeks, still digesting the last conversation with Jerry, mettle grew inside me, strengthening my spirit of independence. The more I thought about his words, the more I began to believe I could exert more control in my life, that there existed different choices. The "how" wasn't yet clear, but I was determined to continue searching.

At the same time, the emotional gap between Richard and me widened. When he was home, we appeared the same on the surface, but underneath the surface we were distant. My goal had shifted from how to fix Richard and my marriage to how to improve my life, and the lives of my two baby girls, whether or not I remained in the marriage.

I decided I would have to take charge of my life. I would have to be the one to raise my standard of living. I would have to be the one to provide a better future for myself and my children.

I just had to figure out how.

Chapter 22
Are You Coming With Me?

January 1966

While standing outside scrubbing laundry in the half-working washing machine, I thought hard about my situation. Even with my newfound determination, escape from the trailer still didn't seem possible.

How can I ever get out of here? I can't qualify for any job that will support the girls and me. But there must be some way out.

Over the next few weeks, the answer slowly formed, almost as if the idea had been handed down from above, but in tiny pieces that had to be assembled to make a complete thought. Since I wasn't qualified for a well-paying job, I needed to get qualified.

I can thank Richard's younger brother, Robert, in large part for showing me a new option. He had started taking college classes in the evenings. The University of Southern Mississippi (USM) in Hattiesburg had recently opened an extension center in Natchez, locally known as the Resident Center. It offered classes in the afternoons and evenings at a local high school.

That's going to be my ticket to a better life. I'll find a way to go to college. Not a quick solution, but the only one that appeared.

Louisiana had no community colleges. The closest college was eighty miles away, in Monroe, far too great a distance to even consider. But the USM Resident Center was right there in Natchez, only ten miles away. It offered only first- and second-year classes, but I couldn't think beyond that anyway. All I knew was the only way I could ever hope to earn enough to support myself was to get more education.

Once the plan had fully taken shape, I felt a sudden urgency to get started. The time had come for me to see how much power I really had.

~~~~~~~

"**Richard, since you've** been working on the river, we have enough money to move into a real house. I want to move to Natchez." I braced for his reaction as I watched him cleaning his fishing gear.

Richard grinned and wobbled his head, gesturing sarcasm, not looking up. "Now, Bet, I can understand why you might to move out of this trailer, but just why do you want to move to Natchez?"

"I've been doing a lot of thinking lately. I've decided to improve my life. The only way to do that is to get an education so I can get a good-paying job. I've decided to go to college—at the Resident Center."

"Little Miss Uppity, are you?" He still didn't look at me.

Uh-oh. Am I ready if he gets angry?

"No. I just want a better life for us and for the girls. The way I see it, the only way to a better life is by getting an education. That's what you said you wanted, too, when we met. Remember your plans to go to college?" My voice speaking so forthrightly sounded strange.

"Yeah, so what? A lot's changed since then."

No matter what he does, I won't stop now.

"You're right. A lot has changed. We have two daughters to raise. I want a better life for them than living here in the cow pasture in an old trailer and being poor."

Richard's eyebrows went up. He looked at me. Just when I thought he might attack, if only verbally, he registered mild surprise as he continued to look into my eyes. I stood firm and looked him square in the eye.

"Okay... so... what if I agree? College costs a lot. And we'd have to pay out-of-state tuition."

"That's my point. If we move to Natchez now, we can meet the six-month residency requirement by the start of fall quarter."

"Are you sure? I thought it was a year."

"Yes, I'm sure. I've checked out everything—the residency requirement, tuition costs, and courses offered."

He suddenly seemed to take more notice. "You're serious about this, aren't you?" He saw a determination in my face he had never seen before. And I saw for the first time how he responded to me when I was firm.

"Yes, I'm very serious. I'd like you to join me, and we can both have a better future. But whether you do or not, I'm going to school."

"But how can we move?"

"Like anybody else. We find a house and we move. We can afford to pay rent now, if we find something modest. And I've saved a little money, maybe enough for deposits."

"You have?" That surprised him even more.

In that brief exchange, I got the smallest taste of power. For over five years, I had needed and depended on Richard, and had been afraid to stand up to him, to exert my own will.

But now, for the first time, I saw that he needed me, too. And I knew that gave me power. I didn't need to hear him say it to know he would agree to the move.

~~~~~

About six weeks later, I surveyed our small, green, three-bedroom house at 2 Brentwood Lane, in a modest, middle-class neighborhood in Natchez. Released at last from the trailer, I could tell people where I lived with no shame, or invite them over without embarrassment. The move initiated a burgeoning growth of strength and determination within me.

On a corner lot, the house included a carport connected to the kitchen by a roomy screened porch, which proved to be a wonderful play area for the girls. We retrieved from the Walkers' the second-hand furniture they had given us soon after we married. They also let us have an old bedroom suite for the girls. They had recently replaced it because it was showing its age and wear, but I welcomed it. My parents donated a few more pieces, including a sofa and chair. Put together, the furnishings weren't exactly in keeping with *House Beautiful*, but it was clean and neat, and a vast improvement over the old, tattered furniture in the trailer.

The Walkers also allowed us to have the piano that had been Richard's when he was a boy. It was in excellent condition, and I saw in that piano a way to earn tuition. Not only would I enjoy playing again, but I could use the years of piano lessons, band, and choir to teach piano to beginning students. As I gained experience, I could potentially take second and third year students, as well.

I started with one girl who lived a few houses away, and slowly added more until I had about eight students. I eagerly saved the few dollars from each one, excited to watch my school fund grow.

I no longer stood in the cow pasture doing laundry half by hand. We now had a fully functioning washing machine—inside yet. With a full-size kitchen, normal-size rooms and decent furnishings, I felt like a regular person. The future still loomed uncertain, but my courage, though still small, was growing, my determination steadfast.

By the start of the fall term in September, Richard had caught some of my ambition, saying he planned to join me in taking college classes. To do that, he had to be in town all the time. So he gave up his job on the river and returned to work for his parents.

Richard's parents, fulfilling a promise they made years earlier, paid his tuition. I had earned enough from teaching piano to pay my tuition for one class, which is all I had the courage to tackle. Even though my confidence in general was growing, I remained unsure of my academic ability. I thought it best to start with something easy. Richard wanted to take the same class I did, and left it to me to choose.

Because the Resident Center was aimed toward adult, part-time students, most of the classes were offered in the evening. This suited us, since that was the only time Richard would be able to attend. I thought it best to start with one of the survey courses required of all students. I didn't want a class on Wednesday because that was choir practice, so I restricted my search to Monday, Tuesday, and Thursday.

I selected Introduction to Psychology—an ironic choice for us both. I chuckled at the possible scenario. Taking that single course would transform Richard into a responsible husband and father, and transform me into the perfect, understanding wife.

Just imagine. One class and our lives will be changed forever!

As the first class meeting drew near, my uneasiness increased. New experiences were usually stressful for me. I remember how nervous I was just opening my first checking account. My apprehension was exacerbated by the stern warnings given by my high school teachers about the difficulty of college. "You think this is difficult, just wait until you get to college. You'll have to work three times as hard."

Richard and I left early, just in case we had a problem finding the correct classroom, me biting my lip all the way. Finding the correct room turned out to be easy, and we soon settled into desks in the back of the room.

I'm not sure what I expected from the class—perhaps a tyrant, a lecture too complex to comprehend, or an impossibly hard assignment. Instead, the teacher was friendly and easy to understand, the lecture clear and thoughtful, and the homework assignment reasonable.

I left class with my fears diminished and my confidence level, while not exactly soaring, no longer on the very bottom rung of the ladder.

~~~~~~

It didn't take long for me to discover the satisfaction of studying and learning, something that had largely eluded me in high school. My unease returned, though, while I waited for the final grades to arrive in the mail. I felt confident when I took the final exam, but I became more doubtful with each day that passed. More than a week later, the grade slips appeared.

Please, oh, please don't be a low grade.

My hand shook as I tore open the envelope. I closed my eyes. I couldn't bear to look. After another whispered prayer, I peeked. My grade was an A. *Wow.* My grades in high school had been mostly Bs and Cs, with only an occasional A.

That single letter transported me through a portal into new territory, one in which I could chart my own course.

Maybe, just maybe, I can do this.

Richard's grade slip was underneath mine. His grade was a B. He was pleased with his grade, although not as excited as I was. Nevertheless, he planned to continue with school, but only one class at a time.

The A emboldened me to register for two classes the next quarter. This time I decided to tackle the basics—English I and Basic College Math.

Richard registered for the English class with me, but about half way through the term, he missed a class because he didn't get home from work in time. He said he was also behind on the homework, so he decided to drop out. At the time, he promised to resume school the next quarter. He never did.

Both classes were enjoyable to me, and I earned two more As. Faith in my capability inched up another small notch. My parents were proud of me, especially Daddy. He had always stressed the value of education, telling me many times, "Learn everything you can. You never know when you'll need it. Besides, knowledge is the one thing no one can take away from you."

Those first successes whetted my appetite for more. I might have gotten a late start, but the desire to take control of my life, achieve my goals, and make up for lost time grew stronger each day.

I began to distance myself from my former life, to be able to see myself not as a helpless victim, but as someone moving forward. I didn't speak about the past to anyone outside the family. The only blight on the new landscape of my life was continued Richard's drinking, although it had abated. Apparently because he seemed to have gained self-respect from the move and his enrollment in school, his binges were less frequent and he hadn't been violent in long time.

April 1967

"**Hey, Bet, I** have an idea." Richard, in his usual seat at the kitchen table, looked up from the paper. He had bathed the girls and put them to bed so I could study. Final exams in the three classes I was taking loomed less than a week away.

Richard had been working hard lately and had been sober for at least six weeks. He said he was proud of my school achievement, although I thought I detected a slight twinge of envy from time to time. Divorce hadn't been on my mind for months.

"Oh, yeah. What's your idea?"

"How about we go camping during the quarter break? The weather's getting nice, and the girls are old enough to make it fun."

A family camping trip did sound nice. Linda was almost two years old and Karen almost four, and we had never had a family vacation. "What kind of camping could we do? We don't have a tent or camping gear. We can't afford to buy all that stuff."

Richard was the eternal optimist. When he was sober, his glasses were rosy-colored. I had heard some of his plans before that were not plausible. I thought of myself as the practical one, the one who saw things as they were rather than the way we wanted them to be. I wanted to see how realistic his plan was before I got excited.

"Tell me what you have in mind."

"I was thinking we could rent a pick-up camper. It would be a lot easier for the kids than tent camping. We can still park in a campground and enjoy the pleasures of being out in nature, but with some conveniences. Rental prices are reasonable."

"That sounds nice. I do prefer running water and soft beds over sleeping on the ground and bathing in cold water. So... where do you want to go?"

"There are some nice campgrounds down around Biloxi. If we camp on the Gulf Coast, we can fish, too."

"Sounds good." The plan did sound all right. I started to share Richard's enthusiasm.

"I'd like to take Robert with us. Do you mind?"

Robert was great with the girls and it would be a little added insurance for Richard, since he was usually on good behavior when with Robert. "I don't mind at all. I'd like to have Robert with us. But when will I have time to prepare for this trip? I have finals coming up, you know."

"I know. I'll do the preparation. Then you'll go?" He looked happier than I had seen him in a long time. Maybe this was just what we needed.

"Yeah, I'll go." I couldn't hold back a big smile.

The girls squealed with excitement when we told them about the trip. They were so eager to go to the beach, they starting planning what they would take. They also started marking off the days on the wall calendar in the kitchen.

~~~~~~

"This looks like a good place." Richard had spotted a clearing in a stand of tall pines just across the road from the beach. Soon after he maneuvered the camper under the tree canopy, we took the girls for their first visit to the ocean. They squealed when the waves lapped over their feet and giggled as they wiggled their toes in the wet sand. Soon they were inspecting the sand for creatures both alive and dead. Robert instructed them in the fine art of making sand castles.

While Robert kept the girls busy, Richard set up a folding table and chairs outside while I cooked inside. By the time dark arrived, we were enjoying our first meal under the stars.

After dinner, Richard and Robert went floundering in the shallow surf, using flashlights and gigs. They failed to spear any fish, but had a great time playing in the surf. They whooped and laughed like kids themselves.

The next day we discovered a segment of an abandoned bridge that had once spanned Biloxi Bay. When a new bridge had been built, only a middle segment of the old one had been removed, which left an abandoned segment on each side of the bay, both now lined with people fishing and crabbing. We found a bait shop nearby and bought crab nets, chicken necks, and two large tubs. Then we parked the camper on one of the old bridge segments.

We tied the chicken necks to the nets and lowered them into the bay. We waited a half hour and checked the nets. Nothing. After another half hour, we had a few small crabs. We used one of the tubs for cleaning the crabs, and other for cooking. Though the crabs were small, we excitedly cleaned and cooked them, a delicacy for all of us. As evening fell, the nets filled quicker and the crabs got bigger. For hours into the night, long after the girls were asleep, we delighted in catching, preparing, and feasting on blue crabs, fresh from the bay.

For three more days, we were a typical American family enjoying a camping vacation. No worries. We fished, crabbed, and played in the surf and sand with the girls.

Something about the freedom of being away from home, or the setting, or the sea air softened my feelings for Richard. He was sweeter and more romantic than he had been in recent months, and I responded with more warmth than had surfaced in a long time. While Robert watched the girls, we enjoyed some time with each other.

Maybe I won't need to get a divorce after all. Judging from this weekend, we're going to be just fine.

Chapter 23
This Time It's Real

The time away had been great, but I returned home eager to embark on another term of school. While unpacking, I glanced at my birth control pill pack. I gasped. I had missed two days in a row, by now going on three.

How could I be so careless? Why did I let myself get so distracted?

I grabbed the pack and rushed to take the two pills, as if the effect would be retroactive.

The signal that the "make-up" pills worked didn't come. Instead, over the next few weeks I experienced queasiness, breast tenderness, bloating, and clearer skin. I didn't need anyone to tell me I was pregnant.

~~~~~~

"Richard, guess what I forgot while we were camping?" We had been back almost a month.

"What?"

"I forgot my birth control pill for two days in a row. I think I'm pregnant." I watched his face closely.

He paused to digest the words. He shrugged and half smiled. "Are you sure?"

"Pretty sure. I have all the usual signs."

"Hmmm. Another chance for a boy, huh?" A faint smile played across his mouth.

"You aren't disappointed?"

"More like surprised. Why, are you?" He looked at me more closely. I couldn't tell him how disappointed I actually was, that I didn't want school to be interrupted, that my plans didn't include having another baby.

"Let's just say I'm happy with two children and hadn't planned on having more. I need some time to get used to the idea."

~~~~~~~~

"If you notice anything unusual, anything at all, be sure to contact me immediately." The doctor seemed to stress *anything* and *immediately,* but then I didn't know him well and dismissed his ominous tone. Dr. Gibson had stopped delivering babies, so I had chosen an obstetrician in Natchez who confirmed I was about six weeks pregnant. He gave me the normal advice about diet, rest, sensible clothing, etc. Maybe he gave this warning to all his patients.

Rita did not want to believe I was pregnant. Apparently she didn't want us to have another child. She pointed to the fact that I wasn't sick like I had been during the first two pregnancies, and didn't show any other visible signs.

How did she know what was going on with my body?

Perhaps she feared having one more person to be ultimately responsible for. She told me to get another opinion, saying she thought maybe something I had some condition that mimicked pregnancy. Ed didn't offer much reaction at all. Clearly, neither of them was happy.

I didn't need another opinion. I knew.

My parents were more accepting, calling it an unexpected blessing. They couldn't completely hide their concern about the added stress another pregnancy posed to all of us, but they had the sensitivity not to verbalize it, overtly showing only support and joy.

I registered for summer classes as planned, grateful the nausea was so mild. Soon after, Richard didn't come home on a Friday night, coming in at about three in the morning, with his usual accusations of "You think you're little miss perfect, etc." But his belligerence failed when fatigue overtook him and he drifted off to sleep instead of fighting.

The next day, when he launched into his usual apology, I couldn't muster the energy to be angry, but I was deeply disappointed. During our camping trip, I had allowed optimism to take hold again. Now my hopes were dashed. I refused to go back to that place of despair, though, so I directed my attention to school, which, I reminded myself, was my way out of the despair for good, my hope for the future.

During neither the July nor August visits did the doctor mention anything unusual, but each time sternly repeated his instruction to contact him right away if I noticed anything out of the ordinary.

The last week in August, during final exams, something out of the ordinary did occur: I started spotting. I called the doctor's office. He came on the line immediately. He listened to my description and then asked me a few questions. Then he commented, "Well, I'm not surprised."

I didn't think much about that at the time, but later realized he must have had some reason to be concerned from the beginning.

The doctor continued, "I want you to go to bed and stay there for at least a week. I want you flat on your back all day. Let me know if the spotting gets worse, or if you notice any other changes."

"Can I get up to go the bathroom?" I tried not to let the worry creep into my voice, but my insides churned. His earlier warnings, coupled with his comment about not being surprised, now added up to something dreadfully wrong.

"Yes, but only for that, and take it slow. And call me every day and tell me what's happening."

To my great surprise, Richard turned into my very own Florence Nightingale, attending to my needs far beyond anything I expected. He started by asking his mother to take the girls. He knew if they were with us, I'd be tempted to take care of them, and they would disturb my rest. He prepared food for us, and ate with me in the bedroom. He kept me supplied with beverages, snacks, newspapers, magazines, and books. He had never been more entertaining as we talked, watched TV, and read.

He did his best at cleaning the house, too. He focused especially on the kitchen, even cleaning out the refrigerator and scrubbing the stove. Not until later did I discover that in his zeal he had used Comet cleanser on the linoleum floor. The grit stubbornly entrenched in the cracks between the tiles lasted through many future cleanings. But he had done his best.

~~~~~

After a week of complete bed rest and pampering, the spotting stopped, and I felt good. In the daily phone call to my doctor, he said I could get up again, but to take it slow and easy. It was a Saturday. I was eager to see the girls, but I didn't want to risk an unfortunate incident with them present. We decided to take me on a "test run," after which, if all went well, we'd go get the girls from Richard's parents. Richard helped me get dressed, and then drove me over to see my parents, carefully avoiding bumps and quick stops.

I felt great when we left the farm a couple of hours later, so we headed directly for the Walkers'. I almost cried at seeing the girls again, and they jumped and squealed in delight at seeing us. They were eager to return home.

That evening, after enjoying the dinner Richard had prepared, all four of us were together in our bed watching TV. Without warning, pain gripped my lower abdomen. Hoping it would go away, I didn't say anything. Richard saw it in my face, though, and looked at me with questioning eyes. "Are you okay?"

I wasn't ready to admit to the degree of the pain. "Yeah, I guess. Probably just tired after my big day out."

Within an hour, though, the pain had become more insistent. I could no longer deny it. "Honey, I'm hurting."

"I knew something wasn't right. I'll bring you some aspirin." He remembered how I loved hot tea when I had cramps, so he brought that and a heating pad.

He put the girls to bed, as tender with them as he had been with me for the last week. Listening to him talking to them so sweetly should have eased the ache, but by the time he returned, the cramping had intensified to a sharp, raw pain. I knew I had to call the doctor. Once again, the doctor wasn't surprised. He phoned a prescription for pain medication to a pharmacy that stayed open late. Richard called his mother to pick it up and bring it to me. By the time she got there, the pain had become almost unbearable. She took the girls back to her house so they wouldn't see me in that condition.

Even with the medication, the excruciating pain was much worse than labor. It felt as though my insides were being ripped into small pieces.

The torment continued throughout the night. By daylight, it began to ease, and I finally went to sleep for a couple of hours, exhausted. When I awoke around eight, I called the doctor, who asked me to meet him at the hospital. He said, "I'm sorry this happened to you, but I'm not surprised. I suspected a flawed pregnancy from the beginning. Nature usually takes care of her mistakes." I was too fatigued and emotionally stunned to ask him to explain more fully.

Richard's devotion accompanied me to the hospital and back home again. We consoled each other as we began to come to terms with the loss. By the end of the two-week ordeal, my love for him had been reborn, as well as a newfound respect.

Following the miscarriage, the sharpness of my grief surprised me. Then the thought came to me that since the pregnancy occurred while I was taking birth control pills, there was a greater risk of an abnormality with the baby. Maybe that's what the doctor was trying to explain.

So in the midst of my pain from losing the infant who had been growing in my womb, a part of me sighed with relief. I accepted the outcome as the hand of fate, realizing that in many ways it was just as well.

Richard agreed that it would have been hard on both of us to have another child, and that it was probably for the best, although he admitted he was more than a little disappointed that we would not have a son.

Chapter 24
Where's Daddy Going?

Early November 1967

"Bettie, what are you going to select for a major?" Bill Gore, the director of the Resident Center, approached me as I entered the office to register for Winter Quarter. "You're going to have to declare one soon, you know. Any ideas?"

His personal interest in my status was surprising. I hadn't realized he was aware that I had not chosen a major yet. "No, Mr. Gore, I haven't. I didn't know I had to decide so soon."

"Come in and have a seat." He half bowed as he swept his arm in the direction of his office. I followed him in and sat in the only guest chair. The limited budget of the Resident Center was evidenced by the size and furnishings of the small office. An old, battered desk sat in the center, behind which stood a single filing cabinet, stacked with files on the top. Beside that more piles of files and books were on the floor. Mr. Gore gave no indication he minded the meager surroundings. His focus appeared to be on teaching and guiding students.

He tented his hands. "You might be interested to know there's a severe teacher shortage right now. There's a new government loan program available to full-time education students that's quite generous. It's called the National Defense Student Loan. For every year you teach, ten percent of the loan is retired, and no repayment is required during that year. So if you teach five years, half the loan is retired and you've had to make no payments." He raised his eyebrows, as if to interest me in the program.

"The load program sounds great. And I guess teaching would be a good job for a mother."

Especially a single mother. But I don't see how I can go to school full-time. Nor do I see how I can complete a bachelor's degree. Maybe someday, if the Resident Center's expanded to four years.

"Okay, let's assume you'll teach. Do you prefer early childhood, elementary, or secondary?" He had started filling out a form.

"I think I'd prefer to teach older kids, so...secondary school."

He smiled as he checked another box and made a note. "Now you need to choose a cognate area. What subject do you want to teach?"

"I'm not sure. I enjoy English grammar and composition, but I don't enjoy some of the literature, especially the ancient selections and most of the poetry. I like science, biology in particular, but I notice there aren't many classes in science offered here."

"No, there aren't. As you know, we rely largely on adjunct instructors. Most of the professionals with advanced degrees in the sciences are doctors, nurses, or other people in the medical field, and few of them have time to teach."

"Well, I've enjoyed the math classes I've had so far." His face brightened; he had taught most of those classes. I remembered Edith Davis, my high school math teacher, who had instilled in me an interest in and appreciation for math. Also, math was mostly reasoning rather than memorizing, which had always appealed to me. "I guess it'll be math."

"An excellent choice," he said with a grin and more marking. "So, it's settled. Math is your major and secondary education is your minor." Mr. Gore suggested which courses I should take, now that I had a more specific goal.

As I walked out of Mr. Gore's office a few minutes later, a realization came over me. No longer a will-of-the-wisp, bending with the direction of the wind, I saw myself more like a young oak tree. A very young one, to be sure, but with the potential to grow taller and stronger. I knew I was laying a foundation for the rest of my life. Regardless of what Richard did, or what happened between us, I was starting to believe I could take care of myself and shape my future.

While my achievement in school gave me strength and confidence, it further widened the gap between Richard and me. When he was sober, he professed respect and admiration at my success in school, although sometimes his words sometimes sounded strained.

Drinking brought his resentment to the surface. Soon after the miscarriage, he had fallen back into his old ways, but with a new twist. He continued to come home drunk and make accusations impossible for me to answer. There were the usual lines I had long ago memorized. But now he added, "You think you're so smart, don't you? You think you're smarter than I am just because you're going to *college*. Well, I'll show you who's smart."

At that point, he usually started fighting, twisting my arm, pushing me, and expressing disdain. His abuse was mild enough that he didn't cause visible bruises, at least not on my face, but it was bad enough to frighten and disgust me.

He continued the next-day apology ritual with the same platitudes I had heard so often before. I had long since stopped trying to figure out what he wanted me to do to help. I just said, "Okay," knowing it was only a matter of time before he repeated the cycle.

One such night, he came home around two in the morning and began to spew his usual accusations louder than usual. I pleaded, "Richard, please be quiet and don't wake the girls. You don't want them to see you like this."

"Why? What's wrong with me? I guess I'm no good because I'm not a college student. Is that it? Are you ashamed of me?"

"No, I'm not ashamed of you. But I don't want you to wake the girls. They'll be scared."

This only increased his agitation. He twisted my arm tightly behind my back. I tried to pull free, but my strength was no match for his.

This time something inside me snapped. Tired of going through these fights, I used the only weapon at hand.

I bit him. Hard.

I had never fought back like that before, and it shocked him momentarily. He let go. Then, in a flash, he spun around and went into the girls' room. Before I could stop him, he picked Karen up and announced, "I'm taking Karen with me. I'll teach you to bite me."

I immediately regretted having fought back.

"Please, don't take her," I begged.

Karen, confused, looked at me with wide, pleading eyes. "Mommy, why is Daddy waking me up?"

"I don't know, sweetie." Then to Richard, "Please, put her down. Can't you see she's scared?"

"No, she's not. She knows Daddy won't hurt her." His grin turned to a vile sneer when he drank. Turning to Karen, he said, "You want to go for a ride with Daddy, don't you?"

She wrinkled her nose at his breath and held out her arms toward me. "I want Mommy."

I didn't dare fight with him while he held Karen. I held out my arms, hoping he would let Karen come to me. Instead, he ignored me, turned and started toward the door, oblivious to the thirty-degree temperature outside. Karen was wearing only a thin nightgown. I grabbed her little pink jacket and ran into the driveway after him.

"At least put her jacket on her."

He ignored me and drove away.

I called the police immediately. "My husband is drunk and just drove away with our three-year-old daughter. She's scared and cold." I gave the dispatcher a description of his truck and the tag number. She reassured me she would broadcast it to every officer in the county.

After the call, I collapsed into a bundle of panic. Pacing, I realized all the education in the world couldn't help me now. I was powerless. Praying the police would find Richard soon, I called Rita. I had no car and would need a way to get Karen.

Twenty minutes later, Rita and I sat at our kitchen table and fretted, drinking coffee and smoking cigarettes, the standard fare during these watches. Within a half hour, the phone made me jump and almost spill my coffee. The police had apprehended Richard. We bundled Linda, half asleep, in a blanket, and headed off to get Karen.

Just inside the police station, I saw Karen in the arms of an officer and wrapped in his jacket. Although she seemed frightened and confused, she appeared to be unharmed. When she spotted me, she squirmed and held out her arms.

The officer gently handed her over and said, "She's cold and scared, but otherwise all right."

How will I ever explain why your Daddy took you off in the middle of the night?

She was three and a half years old, old enough to remember the incident.

~~~~~~~

After that, Karen was much more attentive to Richard's coming and going. When he left, she asked, "Where's Daddy going?" If he didn't return soon, she asked, "Is Daddy late coming home?" If I said, "Yes, he's a little late," she asked, "Mommy, let's go see Mamaw." Or, "Mommy, let's go see Aunt Clarice." Clarice lived across the street and was always kind to us. Even though we never spoke of it, I had the feeling that she had dealt with an alcoholic at some time in her life.

It broke my heart to see my young daughter afraid of her father.

Chapter 25

The Messenger

"How's school going, Bet?" Daddy winked and smiled. By his estimate, his own formal education had not gone past the eighth grade level. His mother died when he was still in elementary school—I think he was eleven—and he was sent to live with an aunt who was also the only school teacher in that rural area. After he and his siblings had attended school several more years, he realized his aunt was simply repeating the same material and he stopped going to school.

Perhaps because he felt deprived of a higher level of education, he placed great value on school. The best he had been able to do was to read a lot, but he said he always regretted that he had not had the opportunity to further his schooling. One of his oft-repeated adages was, "Learn everything you can. You'll never know when it'll come in handy, and knowledge is the one thing no one can take away from you." Therefore, he found vicarious pleasure in my progress in college.

Throughout my childhood, my dad's gentle voice had encouraged me to follow my dreams, never give up, and believe anything was possible. But my mother's voice of doubt and doom was often louder and more persuasive. Richard's blaming me for his drinking only added to my self-doubt. Self-confidence, although increasing, remained low. I still doubted I was capable of making it if I were to get a divorce.

I struggled to strike a balance between honoring my marriage vows and providing a safer and more secure life for my children. Daddy saw that my situation with Richard troubled me, although neither he nor Mother knew the complete story. I didn't tell them about every incident.

One day when I was visiting Daddy, we were standing at the kitchen sink. I was washing dishes and Daddy was making coffee. I can't remember what prompted the discussion, but Daddy started telling me about his early life, a topic he had seldom mentioned.

"You know, Bet, when I married my first wife, I thought I loved her as much as I could love anyone. We seemed happy for several years. But then I found out she was running all over town making debts behind my back, and then I heard from several people that she was running around on me. Over time, she killed all the love I had for her."

"So what happened?"

"I struggled with whether or not to get a divorce. It's against biblical teachings. But I finally came to believe that when all the love is gone, there is no marriage. So I divorced her."

I was surprised that he had been the one who had initiated the divorce. This would have taken place in the 1920s, a time when divorce was unusual—and especially for a husband to divorce his wife.

As we continued talking that day, he said, "I know you must be struggling to decide what to do. I'm just saying that I believe when all the love is gone, there is no marriage." I interpreted that as his way of giving me his permission to get a divorce. Or, at the very least, telling me that if I made that choice, he would understand.

~~~~~~

Even though I was worn out from Richard's repeated bouts of drinking, and even though Daddy had indicated it would be a reasonable choice, I still lacked the conviction that divorce was the right thing to do.

Marriage vows echoed in my head. And right before my eyes stood an example of someone holding onto a marriage in the face of extreme trials and emotional hardship: Rita. She remained a strong influence, often telling me, "It takes two to fight." After many of Richard's binges, she acted as if he and I were equally responsible for his conduct. She encouraged me to accept Richard's behavior, and regularly reminded me of the vows I had taken, especially "for richer or poorer, in sickness and in health."

While the debate raged on in my head, I continued to make progress in school. Whether I stayed in the marriage or not, continuing my education remained a high priority. In either case, I wanted to provide a better life for my daughters and myself.

Late November 1967

A sharp knock on the door of the classroom interrupted the lecture in world history. A young man opened the door. As I heard him ask for Bettie Walker, I spotted Rita standing behind him.

What's going on? What's Rita doing here?

She motioned for me to come out.

I asked, "What's wrong?"

"Bettie, there's been an accident. You need to come with me—now."

My heart jumped into my throat. "What kind of accident?" We rushed toward her car.

"It's your dad. He's fallen."

Oh, no.

"What happened? How bad is it?"

Rita paused, which made my stomach tighten. "I don't know. All I was told is that we need to get there right away." She didn't look at me.

My mind raced with possibilities. For years, Mother had worried that Daddy would fall or injure himself somewhere on the farm, away from the house, and be unable to call for help. Countless times when he was late coming home, she envisioned him lying in a remote part of the farm, badly injured and in pain. We had heard her conjectures so many times I thought I was numb to that sort of worry. But it had been dark for almost two hours. He should have been in the house long before now.

Rita was quiet and tense during the drive to my parents. She said more than once, "We'll know more when we get there."

Too many cars crowded the driveway. Some I recognized, such as the Schaffner's from down the road. Most I didn't.

Panic rose up through my chest and sent a chill through me as I went in the back door. From the kitchen, I heard low, somber voices coming from the next room. As I entered the living room, I saw Mother's face.

No words were needed. The agony on her face told me it was the worst possible news—he was gone. For just a moment, she looked at me with pleading eyes, as if I could somehow make it better. Then she rushed over and clung to me, sobbing, "At least he went suddenly. He didn't suffer." We stood holding each other as the news sank in, tears stinging my face.

When finally able to speak, I asked, "When did it happen?"

"Late this afternoon. He wasn't here when I got home from work. I called and called, then I rang on the post." When we wanted to signal Daddy to come to the house, we beat a signal on a metal post in the carport.

"When he didn't answer and didn't come home, I went for help. Mr. Schaffner found him only a little way from the house. He had paper sacks with him to pick up pecans."

"What happened?" I was still in shock.

"Doctor Gibson said it was a cerebral hemorrhage. At least he didn't suffer. You know how often he prayed to go suddenly." Only then did I recognize Dr. Gibson, our long-time family physician, standing in the corner.

Dr. Gibson agreed with mother's sentiment, "Yes, his prayer was definitely answered. He probably didn't even know what was happening and certainly didn't feel any pain."

I remembered how often I'd heard him say, half jokingly, half seriously, "If I get so I can't take care of myself, just knock me in the head and throw me in the river." He valued his quality of life and didn't want to be around if he was no longer physically active and mentally alert. Because he was sixty-two when I was born, I had been warned for years I could lose him at any time. I was told how lucky I was to have had him as long as I had. It was hard for me to think of him as old, though, because he looked and acted so much younger than his years—and his peers.

Just the same, I wasn't ready to lose Daddy. Not yet. I still needed time to absorb more of his faith. I needed to learn more of his wisdom. Mother had never shown the same thoughtful insight into our human behavior as Daddy had. It was his quiet, constant love and support that had seen me through the dark days of living in the cow pasture. And even though I didn't comprehend it at the time, his advice would guide me for the rest of my life.

~~~~~

Losing my dad left me feeling very alone; my insecurity resurfaced. Would I make the right decision regarding my marriage? Would I be able to complete my degree? Was I a fit mother? So many doubts remained.

Yet, in a different way, Daddy's loss also brought new hope. Richard said he respected Daddy more than anyone he had ever known. He expressed overwhelming sorrow for all the times he had disappointed Daddy and said he intended to redouble his effort to live up to my dad's standards. Seeing Richard so deeply moved caused me to hope—yet one more time—that "the big change" would take place.

April 1968

"What did you think about that last passage?"

Sharon, a fellow student in my English literature class, had come over on a Saturday afternoon to study with me. We were preparing for a big test scheduled for the following week.

Richard was working in the oil field with Robert. Karen and Linda were playing quietly in their room—at least quietly enough to not disturb our studying. Late in the afternoon, Karen came into the kitchen and asked, "Where's Daddy?"

"He's working, sweetie. He'll be home soon." The look on her face told me she was worried about him coming home intoxicated again. The effect of my dad's death had worn off, and he had returned to his old ways.

"Can we go to Mamaw's anyway?" The concerned look on her face was much too serious for a child of four.

"We'll see." As Karen walked away, Sharon looked at me quizzically.

I offered, "Sometimes after work, he stops for a beer. Karen doesn't like to be around him when he's been drinking."

Sharon's face showed her skepticism of my explanation. "I think I understand how she feels. My dad was an alcoholic. I remember the dread and fear of him coming home drunk."

"Your father was an alcoholic?"

"Yes, he was, although I don't tell many people. You can probably understand why."

"Yes, I do understand. To tell you the truth, I think Richard's an alcoholic."

"Oh, I know all about the isolation and trying to hide it from people. I rarely brought friends to my house because I was afraid my dad might be drunk and embarrass me."

I was suddenly interested in what it was like to be the child of an alcoholic. "That must have been difficult."

"Yes, it was. We didn't want to leave Mom, because we had this idea we could protect her. Looking back now, I realize what a big responsibility that was for us kids. I was the second of four. When my big brother got older, Dad started hitting him, too. Luckily, he never came after me." Pain covered her face, the memories darkening her eyes.

Will Karen have that look when she's an adult and remembering her childhood?

Suddenly she seemed to snap back to the present and her face relaxed. "The happiest day of my life was the day Mom decided to leave him. One night when he was drunk and belligerent, threatening to kill Mom, she whispered to us. 'Quick. Gather up as much as you can, and get in the car.' She had recently located a shelter for abused women, and had prepared us for a possible escape.

"We knew this was it. Mom distracted Dad while we kids grabbed our things and slipped out of the house unnoticed by him. A few minutes later, Mon rushed out and we took off. We went directly to the shelter, where we stayed for a few days until we could safely leave town.

"With only the little we had been able to take, which wasn't much, we started over. Mom worked as a waitress, so we were dirt poor. My brother and I were old enough to work part-time, too, but we still never had enough. But in spite of the struggle for money, we were happier than we'd ever been because we were free from the verbal and physical abuse."

I wasn't quite sure what to say, but I hoped there was a good end to the story. "Whatever happened to your dad?"

"He's old and sick now, but he's finally sober."

"How did he get sober?" I hoped to hear about a magical solution.

"At first, Mom was afraid he would try to find us and harm her, so she was afraid to contact anyone who knew him. We had moved to another town, and didn't want him to know where. But after several years had passed, she asked an old friend about him and found out he'd started going to AA. He had ended up in the emergency room one night, and was told he was lucky he had hadn't died, and that if he didn't stop drinking, he *would* die. The doctor told him he need to get help."

"How awful."

"That probably saved his life, though."

"Have you seen him recently?"

"Once. He's really sad now. I feel sorry for him and all, but I still remember what he did to us and to Mom. I go to Al-Anon once in a while to try to sort out my feelings about him."

"What's Al-Anon?"

"It's a support group for spouses, other family, and friends of alcoholics."

"Thank you, Sharon. I know it must have been hard for you to tell me all of this, but I really needed to hear what it's like from a child's point of view. I've been wrestling with whether or not to leave Richard. I don't want to desert him if I can help him. And if alcoholism is a disease, then staying with him comes under the heading 'in sickness and in health.' But I also have to consider my children. As you can see, Karen is already affected."

Sharon said, "I understand your struggle. I certainly don't want to influence your decision. I can only tell you what a relief it was when we left my dad."

"Well, you've given me a lot to think about."

Sharon added, "If you want other people to talk to, or just want to hear how other family members cope with living with an alcoholic, I recommend Al-Anon."

I had heard the saying, "When the student is ready, the teacher will appear." Sharon brought the message I needed to hear just when I needed to hear it. We didn't have any other classes together and soon drifted apart. But her story remained with me.

The psychiatrist at the state mental hospital had recommended Al-Anon years earlier. I didn't go then.

Maybe now it was time.

Chapter 26
Pauline

When I had told Richard—demanded really—that I wanted to move to Natchez, he had agreed. I had been surprised to see that I had that much power. I decided to test it once again.

"Richard, Sharon told me what it was like growing up with an alcoholic father. She says he finally stopped drinking when he started going to AA meetings. And she told me about Al-Anon, a support group for friends and family of alcoholics. I think you need AA and I need Al-Anon."

"I'm not going to any AA meeting, you hear? I'm not a drunk."

"You keep saying you're not going to drink anymore, but you keep doing it. If you're not an alcoholic, then why can't you stop drinking?"

"I could stop if I wanted to. What's wrong with having a few drinks once in a while?"

"Richard, you have more than a few drinks. You have way too many, and you spend too much money when you do. Then you fight with me. You keep saying you're going to do better, but you don't. You even took Karen in the middle of the night. You think that's all okay? You think that's normal?"

The mention of Karen, his cherished first-born, hit a nerve. I could see his face soften. The day after he took her, she was cool and distant to him. It broke his heart. Humiliated, he couldn't even look her straight in the face. But young children are resilient and, in a short time, she was back in his arms, laughing at his playful teasing—but only when he was sober.

The reminder of that incident cut through his defenses, if only for a moment. "Is this some kind of ultimatum?"

"Don't think of it as an ultimatum. Think of it as a chance to hold our marriage together."

He frowned slightly as his eyes searched my face for some clue of how serious I was. My resolve must have shown, because he reluctantly agreed to attend an AA meeting while I went to an Al-Anon meeting.

~~~~~

We weren't sure we had found the right place when we drove up. The address matched the one we had been given, but the house sat in a run-down neighborhood and looked as if had faced hard times. But there were more cars there than any family I knew about.

Richard said, "This doesn't look right. I think we should leave."

Neither of us knew what to expect, and I had always hated facing the unknown, but I couldn't turn back. "Wait just a minutes."

Just then, a smiling face appeared outside the car window. A woman asked, "Are you looking for AA? Or Al-Anon?"

"Yes," Richard said.

I said, "Both."

"Well, this is the place. I'm Virginia. Come on in. I promise we won't bite." She chuckled at her own wit.

Virginia asked which meetings we wanted. Seeing the hesitation on Richard's face, I answered, "He's looking for AA, and I'm looking for Al-Anon."

She pointed Richard toward the AA room and took me into the Al-Anon room. I accepted the offered coffee from an industrial-size coffeemaker sitting on a rickety, folding table in one corner of the room. The only other furnishings were an assortment of old folding chairs, loosely arranged in a circle.

Looking around, I saw mostly women in their thirties and forties. Of the twenty or so people, only a few were in their late teens and twenties, and two were men. I wondered if they were husbands or parents of an alcoholic. As more people trickled in, warm greetings ensued, indicative of long-standing friendships.

First one, then another, gave reports such as, "I've had a good week, so far," or "He was drunk most of the week, but he pretty much left me alone. I'm grateful for that." One said, "He disappeared for three days this week. I just wish he'd tell me ahead of time, so I could make some plans of my own." Everyone laughed.

The humor was unexpected in a situation so serious.

Virginia asked me to introduce myself and tell why I was there. "I'm... Bettie and... uh, I think my husband might be an alcoholic."

"Uh-huh. You think he *might* be an alcoholic." It was the woman who appeared to be in charge of the group. "We all wondered that at one time, honey. How long have you been thinkin' he *might* be an alcoholic?" Pleasantly round, with a rough voice, she radiated both compassion and no-nonsense honesty. She reminded me of my friend Willese from the trailer park, exuding the same warmth and nurturing spirit. Someone called her Pauline.

"Well, he's had some kind of problem for years." I stopped picking at a hangnail and folded my hands as I took in a deep breath. "He doesn't drink all the time. He'll go for several weeks, or sometimes even months, without drinking at all. And then he'll stop on the way home from work for one beer—only he never stops with just one. Sometimes he comes home the same night, and sometimes he's gone for a day or two. He's always sorry after he's sobered up. And when he's not drinking, he's usually great."

"How many of us have heard those sincere apologies?" Pauline asked the group.

"Most of us." "I have." "Me." The comments came from all over the room.

"Honey, whut you got yourself is a binge alcoholic. He's prob'ly real sincere when he's doin' all that apologizin'. But the alcohol has control of him. We've all seen it. Everyone here knows someone bein' controlled by alcohol. Some of 'em drink every day, some of 'em go on binges. You're not by yourself, honey."

A binge alcoholic. That sounds right.

As I listened to others talk about their experiences, I didn't want to admit my life was as wretched as theirs. Mine certainly wasn't as bad as the young woman who bore on her arms and face the bruises she had recently received from her husband. With tears streaking down her face, she asked, "What should I do? He says if I leave, he'll come after me. I'm scared he will."

One of the men urged her to call him anytime she needed help.

Pauline said, "Honey, as long as you stay with him, we'll help you any way we can. But if you decide to leave, I promise we'll find a safe place for you. Right, group?"

"Yeah." "You bet." "Sure thing."

"But he doesn't mean to hurt me. He just gets so angry when he drinks. He's always sorry afterward. He loves me, I know he does."

"Honey, they all love us. Just listen to 'em tell us how much they love us. And they never mean to hurt us. Ask anybody here. Just 'cause he doesn't mean to do it and just 'cause he really loves you don't mean it don't hurt, does it? It don't keep you from being scared, and it don't guarantee you won't get hurt even worse next time."

"But I love him." Her voice dripped with desperation.

Pauline said, "We know you do, honey. I sure can't tell you how to feel, and I ain't tryin' to. I'm just tellin' you what to expect. As long as you stay with him, you gotta know what to expect."

At that moment, Richard barged in. "Come on, Bettie. We're leaving." Embarrassed, but somehow knowing everyone in the room understood, I got up and followed him out.

Richard marched out to the car. "Look, I told you I didn't need to come here. I ain't no alcoholic, I ain't no drunk. I'm not like those drunks in there. I don't need to come here and listen to people talk about waking up not knowing where they were, or being falling-down drunk, or sleeping in the street, or none of that stuff."

I waited a moment. "Are you finished?"

"Yeah. I'm just telling you I'm not coming back here again, so don't ask me."

"Okay, I won't. But I'm coming back to Al-Anon. I want to hear more. You may not think so, but I'm more convinced than ever you *are* an alcoholic. If you ever decide you want help, you know where to find it. Until then, I can't help you. No one can."

Richard sulked during the drive, and for the rest of the evening, but by the next day, he acted as if the evening hadn't happened.

All day I thought over what I'd heard at the meeting. Before that, I couldn't imagine other lives being like ours. Even though I wasn't happy to learn of other people's difficulties, I was somehow comforted to know I wasn't alone, that Richard's behavior wasn't unique. I also thought about Pauline's advice to the young woman.

If you stay, we'll help you. But you gotta' know what to expect.

I looked forward to the next meeting.

The next week, I wasn't nearly as nervous as I entered the meeting room. Once again Pauline took charge, compassionately dispensing advice. The young woman from the week before wasn't there. I worried about her. Had she been hurt again? Worse? Had she left? Could she be caught up in the same sort of limbo as me, miserable but unable to break free?

Someone asked Pauline how she coped with her husband. "Oh, I left Charlie five years ago. Never been better in my life. He's still trying to kill hisself with the alcohol, and I feel bad about that, but there's nothing I can do for him, and I'm not gonna let him ruin me."

"Why do you still come to the meetings?"

She raised her eyebrows. "I keep coming here hoping I can help somebody else. This group saved my life. Made me understand my choices. Gave me the courage to leave him. I might be dead by now if I hadn't. Charlie could be awfully mean."

I asked, "Can alcoholics ever stop drinking? Do they ever change?"

"Oh, some do. The ones who admit they're sick and ask for help. But they have to really mean it. And if they don't want help, there's not a thing anybody else can do for 'em."

She looked straight at me and added, "Honey, I can see the misery in your face. Let me see if I can tell what you're thinking. You're thinking he's gonna have some miraculous change any day now, 'cause every time he sobers up he says he's gonna do better. Well, listen to me good. You could be an old woman before he changes, if he ever does. You need to take a good, hard look at him just the way he is right now. If you want to stay with him, just like he is, we'll stand by you and do everything we can to help you. But if you don't want him just like he is, you need to be making plans to leave."

Pauline didn't beat around the bush; she told it as she saw it. Even though I didn't know it at that exact moment, I needed to hear her words. They echoed in my head over the next few weeks just like Sharon's had, even as I resisted the truth of them. Slowly, as I thought over the last seven years, Pauline's words seemed true.

Richard might never change.

Chapter 27

Miss Perfect Makes a Decision

Summary, 1968

*D*oes God speak through angels? Angels posing as ordinary people? Could it be that He has been trying to answer my prayers?

I asked Daddy what I should do, as if his spirit could hear me. I listened as if I actually expected him to answer and give me his ever-wise advice. It never came, or I was unable to recognize it if it did.

I prayed for guidance. I had given up on my original request that God "make" Richard change his behavior. After I fully grasped the concept of free will—that we aren't puppets—I saw the flaw in my request. So I had changed my prayer, now asking how I should deal with Richard just as he was. Still, I didn't hear God's voice.

Then I wondered if perhaps He had been speaking to me, using people like Sharon. And Pauline.

~~~~~~

On a Saturday afternoon in early October, housecleaning day, I listened to Karen, in her bedroom playing happily with her dolls. Hearing her talk to her dolls in her "Mommy" voice evoked an irrepressible smile. I looked out the kitchen window to see Linda riding her Marvel the Mustang, a riding horse on wheels, in the carport. After confirming that she wasn't wheeling down into the street, I smiled at the sight of her riding so freely.

I leaned into the tub with a scrub brush in one hand and cleanser in the other.

Soon after I started scrubbing, I heard the back door open suddenly, too forcefully for it to be Linda. I rushed from the bathroom to see Richard holding Linda, and locking the kitchen door behind him. After he put Linda down, he knelt beside her and, in a syrupy-sweet voice, told her to go to her room and play with her sister. Amazingly, for a child as strong-willed as Linda, she did as he asked. The red eyes, sneer, disheveled clothes, and unmistakable odor of whiskey already permeating the room told me he had been drinking—and more than just a little.

Brushing past me, he marched into the spare bedroom near the living room, the "junk room" as we called it. Not everything in it was junk, though. This room also held Richard's guns: the twelve-gauge shotgun he'd fired in the trailer years ago, a thirty-ought-six with a scope, a twenty-two rifle, and a twenty-two handgun. From the hall, I saw him pick up the twenty-two pistol and load it.

What is he thinking? And why haven't I insisted he remove his guns?

I never knew what he intended to do at that moment, because a knock on the back door interrupted him. I rushed to the door, glad to have someone else there, hoping the interruption would deter Richard from his goal. It was highly unlikely Richard would make threats to anyone outside the family. Approaching the door, I saw Robert through the glass.

I unlocked the door. Cocking his head to one side, Robert smiled as he asked, "Why was the door locked? Afraid of burglars in the middle of the day?"

"No, your brother locked it," I whispered.

Robert still didn't catch on that something was wrong. "I came to get some venison from your freezer. Dad wants to barbeque tomorrow." Richard had killed a deer the year before and we had filled the freezer on the back porch with venison. About half remained.

As Robert stepped into the kitchen, he spotted Richard coming from the other direction with the pistol in his hand. He must have seen Richard's condition, too. "Aw, Richard, what do you think you're doing? Put the gun away."

"Who are you to tell me what to do?" Richard swayed a bit.

"I'm your brother, and I know you don't need a gun here in the house."

"You don't know nothin'. You don't know what it's like to be married to Little Miss Perfect here. You don't know what it's like for everybody to think you're a drunk just 'cause you have a few drinks. So just shut up." Gesturing with the pistol, he said, "Both of you. Go sit in the living room."

We obeyed. I sat on the end of the sofa nearest the kitchen, and Robert sat across from me in a small chair. Richard remained near the doorway from the kitchen to the living room. My brain tried to figure out what he might have in mind. My heartbeat drummed in my ears, and I wished I could silence it.

The girls were still playing in their room, apparently unaware of the tension in our end of the house. I heard a familiar, "Stop. You're messing up my doll." It was Karen, fussing at Linda. "Give her to me. I want her."

Linda responded, "No, wait. I want to put this dress on her."

Richard looked in their direction; they had gotten his attention, too. I asked him, "Richard, please let me go see about the girls." I got up slowly, watching for his reaction as I walked in front of him. He didn't stop me.

I went quickly to quiet their squabble. Kneeling, I said, "Girls, listen to me. This is important. I want both of you to be very quiet. Daddy's upset, and we don't want to make him any worse."

I stopped to listen as I watched the girls' faces. Their eyes widened as they nodded, as if they understood the gravity of what I had said.

I hoped Richard was facing away from my direction as I seized what appeared to be an opportunity. I slipped across the end of the hallway into our bedroom. I dialed the memorized number for the police and whispered into the phone, "I'm at 2 Brentwood Lane.

My husband's drunk and he's holding my two daughters, his brother, and me at gunpoint—"

Richard jerked the phone out of my hand. He threw it across the room, ripping the wires out of the wall.

I sighed deeply. I had seen him like this far too many times. "Richard, please don't be like this. You don't want the girls to see you this way, do you?"

"I don't give a damn how they see me. You've already poisoned their minds against me anyway. Haven't you, Trinkatunia?" A familiar look of revulsion contorted his face.

"No, I haven't. Look, at least let me take them to Clarice's. Whatever you intend to do, you don't want to harm them."

He stood thinking for a minute. "All right, you can take them over there. But I'm warning you, if you don't come right back, I'm coming after you."

As Richard stalked back to the living room, I returned to the girls' room, hoping they would agree to come with no argument. "Girls, come with me quickly. We're going to Aunt Clarice's."

Their faces told me I would have no resistance. Karen understood Daddy was drunk again, and Linda took her cue from Karen. I lifted Linda onto my hip and took Karen's hand. We slipped quietly through the living room and out the front door. Only after we were outside and half across the front lawn did I dare breathe again.

I pounded on the door. "Clarice? Are you here?"

What will I do if she's not home?

Clarice opened the door, laughing, "I'm coming. Lordy mercy, what's the big emergency?"

"Actually, Clarice, this *is* an emergency. Richard's drunk and threatening us. I got him to let me bring the girls over here. Will you watch them?"

Suddenly serious, "Of course. I'd do anything for these sweet little girls."

"And Clarice, will you call the police? I tried, but Richard yanked the phone out of the wall in the middle of the call. I don't know if they got the address or not."

"Of course."

If Robert hadn't still been in the house, I would have stayed at Clarice's and risked Richard coming after me. I'd never known him to inflict his violence on anyone outside the family. And I knew he liked Clarice and Jim a lot, so I doubted he would embarrass himself in front of them. But I didn't know what he might do to Robert if I didn't return, so I went back.

Richard opened the front door as I approached it, and then locked it after I was in. He drew the curtains in the living room and closed the blinds in the kitchen, still giving no indication of what he intended. I searched his face for clues.

Is he holding us as hostages, or does he intend to hurt us?

Apparently unsure himself of his next move, Richard paced unsteadily around the small living room, while Robert and I cowered together on the couch, apprehensively watching and waiting, willing ourselves to stay calm. Ten minutes passed.

The pacing stopped when we heard a car pull into our driveway. Curious, Richard peeked through the curtains momentarily, but then pulled back and closed them quickly. Moments later a knock on the door was accompanied with, "Open up. Police."

Richard yelled back, "I'm not opening the door. I've got a gun, so don't try anything."

"Who's in there with you? What is it you want?"

"My wife and my little brother." His words were slurred and he wobbled as he tried to straighten up.

"Are they all right?"

"Yeah, they're fine." *Fine physically maybe, but a wreck emotionally.*

"Okay, son, why don't you tell me what you want?"

"First, don't call me 'son.' I ain't your goddamn son! In fact, I'm not much of anybody's son. At least that what *they'd* prob'ly say." His face shifted slightly from pure anger to a mixture of sullenness and resentment.

"What's your name?" the officer yelled.

"Richard. My name's Richard."

"Richard, what do you want?"

He paused for a minute, then he answered, "I want you to get my mother over here."

Of course he does. He always turns to her when he's in trouble.

"Why do you want your mother over here?"

"'Cause she's the reason I'm so screwed up. She ought to get a good look at what she's done to her little boy."

Well, this is a first. I've never seen him blame his mother. For once, I'm not his target.

The officer asked, "Where is she? How do I get her over here?"

"Her number's six five four zero four three eight. You call her, she'll come over."

No response from the officer, but I heard police radios, voices of officers, and additional voices in the background, ones I suspected belonged to inquisitive neighbors. It sounded as if at least one more police car had arrived. As I heard passing traffic slow to a crawl, I imagined drivers gawking. My cheeks flushed. I wished our house wasn't on a busy street.

Inside, the only sound was Richard's boots as he stalked in circles around the small room, muscles in his jaws flinching. He reached into his jacket pocket, pulled out a flask of whiskey, took a big drink, and screwed up his face in response.

Just what he needs. Or... maybe it really is what he needs. Maybe he'll drink enough to pass out.

Robert begged, "Come on, Richard, why are you doing this? Put down the gun. You don't want to shoot Bettie or me."

"Shut up. You're another one who thinks you're so good. You're Mama's favorite 'cause you don't do nothin' wrong."

Another few minutes passed, then another car stopped. Shortly, Rita's voice barked through the front door. "Richard, what are you doing? What do you want?"

He laughed as he yelled back, "Well, hey, Mama. Just who I want to come in and join the party. I want you to get a real good look at what you've done to me."

Rita answered, "Richard, I'll come in, but only if you let Robert and Bettie leave. Will you do that?"

He looked over at us, steadying the hand with the pistol, tightening his grip. His eyelids drooped as he said, "Yeah, I'll let 'em go." Using the gun to direct us, he motioned us to the door. "I'm turning the lock, but I've still got the gun on 'em, so don't nobody try anything. No cops up close."

He unlocked the door, opened it slowly, and peeked out. Seeing there were no officers nearby, he grabbed his mother's arm and pulled her inside before he pushed Robert and me out. When we were outside, we heard the lock click back into place.

The spectacle on the front lawn included three police cars and at least six officers. Two officers rushed to Robert and me and looked us over. Satisfied we were all right, they took us to the edge of the yard and asked, "What's his problem? What do you think he wants?"

"He wouldn't tell us what he wanted," I answered.

A nervous officer asked, "Do you think he'll hurt his mother?"

Robert huffed an answer. "No. His problem is he's drunk. I have no idea what he wants, but he won't hurt Mom."

I added, "If anyone can talk him out of the gun, it's her. She's the only one he listens to when he's drunk."

"He's done this before?"

"Not exactly, but similar. Sometimes when he drinks, he gets angry and makes threats. He's never wounded me seriously, though." I remembered the near-miss when he fired the shotgun in the trailer. I had convinced myself that he'd never do anything like that again, but now I wondered how long before that changed.

I looked across at Clarice's and hoped she had the girls in the back of the house. I didn't want this scene to be among their childhood memories.

I lost all sense of time as we waited in the front yard, providing the afternoon's entertainment to the neighbors. I yearned to become invisible, or just melt into the grass. My jaws ached from clenching my teeth.

Finally, Rita and Richard emerged, Rita holding the gun. As if I didn't exist, Rita talked to the officers and convinced them to let her take Richard home with her. The officers never so much as glanced my way, but agreed to her request.

The humiliating scene in our front yard brought my life into focus much like adjusting the lens on a camera. My decision was now crystal clear. Days such as this didn't belong in my daughters' futures. They deserved better. I would get a divorce. Maybe not immediately, but soon.

In the midst of the chaos, calm descended over me.

Chapter 28
The Appointment

November 1968

What had started as an emotional crack between Richard and me had widened to a chasm. When he launched into his apologies, I felt no hurt, no anger, no pity, and offered no agreement to "help" him. I had developed a near-numbness to anything other than the desire to escape my roller-coaster life. I wasn't sure if I simply didn't love Richard anymore, or if my emotions had shut down out of self-protection. It didn't really matter. His charisma and endearments that had enabled me to forgive him and keep trying had finally vanished. Now when I looked at him, I felt nothing.

Nothing good, nothing bad. Just nothing.

Richard sensed the distance—I saw the hurt on his face. How could he not see it when I didn't react to his caresses and kisses? When I avoided intimacy? He wasn't brave enough to talk about it, though. He pretended not to notice, as if by pretending everything was the same as before, it would still be so.

Having at last made the decision to get a divorce, I waited for the right time to make my move. I reasoned it would be smart to complete two more quarters of school if I could. Then I would have most of the core curriculum completed and almost two years' credits. After a divorce, working full-time would be necessary, and I wanted to get a few more difficult courses completed before that. Also, I hoped the more credit hours I earned, the better job I would be able to get. So I concentrated on completing the current quarter and hoped I could get through one more without Richard doing anything too drastic.

~~~~~~

In the Resident Center office in late November, I scanned the course offerings for Winter Quarter. Only one class on the list counted toward my major—Calculus II, the second in the series of three classes. Even though I was disappointed there weren't more classes available, it turned out just as well because it was my most difficult class so far, requiring a great deal of study.

By the end of January, Richard's extra-long run of good behavior almost lulled me into thinking there was no need to rush into the upheaval of divorce. The Christmas season had come and gone with Richard stone cold sober throughout—the first time in our marriage. He surprised me with a dishwasher, the most generous gift he had ever given me. I looked it as an offering of atonement, a plea to not leave him. It was a portable, meaning it was on rollers and connected to the kitchen faucet with a hose. A good choice for old houses like ours, ones not designed for a dishwasher.

As if Richard sensed he was on his last chance, he tried extra hard to be kind and helpful. He watched the girls while I studied, helped with the cooking, and wore the forced smile of feigned contentment.

Even though I knew the peace wouldn't last, it wasn't in me to pull the rug out from under him while he was trying so hard. I needed a reason to act. I waited for the inevitable "fall from the wagon." I didn't have to wait long. It came at the end of January.

We had a late breakfast that Sunday, after which the girls went to their room to play, leaving Richard and me to have a second cup of coffee over the Sunday paper. Mid-afternoon, Richard said, "I think I'll go to the store and get some steaks for dinner tonight. With baked potatoes and that great bread you made yesterday, we'll have a nice dinner."

Soon after he left, I scrubbed the potatoes and prepared a marinade for the steaks. Then I started on homework.

Hmm. Five o'clock. He should be home by now. How long can it take to buy meat?

Darkness fell. No Richard.

I was certain he was drinking. Karen looked up with a much-too-serious look for one so young, and in a soft, plaintive voice asked, "Can we go see Mamaw?"

"Let's call and see if it's okay."

I called Rita. "Richard went out this afternoon to buy steaks, and he's long overdue coming home. Karen wants to know if we can come over." I didn't need to say anymore.

"Of course, all my girls can come over." This was an old, tired story for her, too.

Rita made snacks for the girls, whose attention was captivated by the Walkers' new color TV. By around ten, the girls were tired, and I didn't want to stay overnight, so we risked going home. Karen's fatigue had overtaken her worry, and she and Linda were soon fast asleep. I stayed up a little longer, finally getting into bed around midnight. But every small sound made my eyes pop open. Around three o'clock, I heard Richard drive into the carport.

I lay there listening.

How far gone is he this time?

He stumbled his way into the bedroom. I pretended to be asleep. That didn't matter to Richard. He shook me until I could no longer fake sleep. He began with his usual you-think-you're-so-perfect speech. When I tried to calm him, he became more agitated. He grabbed my arm and twisted it behind my back.

I looked at him squarely and, through clenched teeth, said in a low, steady voice, "We...will...not...fight—not tonight. Let me go." I had wanted to say that to him many times before, but didn't have the resolve. This time I found the courage. My firmness somehow pierced the alcohol haze, because he slowly released my arm and backed away. "Now just go to sleep, and we'll talk tomorrow."

He muttered under his breath as he did it, but he obediently undressed and collapsed into bed. He fell asleep in no time.

Thank you, Richard, for backing down and not hurting me. And thank you for giving me the excuse I've been waiting for. Now I can make my move.

A certain satisfaction carried me into sleep.

At nine o'clock Monday morning, I called the office of John Tipton, the lawyer I had already chosen. I made an appointment for two o'clock. *Perfect.*

Around ten thirty, Richard woke up. I waited until he had showered and had coffee before calmly saying, "Richard, I need you to do something for me." He looked weary, defeated, and didn't look at me. He didn't even begin to apologize.

"What is it, Bet?" Even though he hadn't said the words, his face had apology written all over it.

"I need you to stay with the girls this afternoon."

The apologetic look turned into a puzzled look. "Okay, but why?"

"I have an appointment to see a lawyer."

"A lawyer. Why?"

"I'm going to file for divorce."

His body deflated. He looked down and nodded his head slightly, as if he had known he would hear these words sooner or later. He finally looked up at me with pleading, desperate eyes. "Bet, please don't do this. I know I've messed up again, but I'll do anything you want. I can't make it without you."

"I'm sorry, Richard, but I've heard your promises over and over." My voice was flat, matter-of-fact. "I won't live like this anymore, always wondering if you're going to come home drunk again, if you're going to try to hurt me—or the kids."

Richard pleaded, "Bet, believe me, I'll really try this time. Please give me another chance."

"That's just it. For seven years I've given you chances. Yesterday afternoon, Karen asked to go to see Mamaw. She does this now because she's afraid to be here when you get home. I don't want my children to grow up afraid of their father."

He winced and looked down. "There's no way I can talk you out of this, is there?"

"Look, I'm not doing this to hurt *you*. I'm doing it *for* the girls and for me. We deserve better. I've made up my mind."

He took a deep breath and looked down again. He could see I wouldn't back down. "Okay, I'll stay with them. What will you tell them?"

"I'll tell them I have to go somewhere for a while. No need to upset them."

"How long will you be?"

"I don't know. Why? Are you so busy you can't stay with your children for an hour or so?" My impatience sprang more from my nervousness than anything else. This action, anticipated for months, would change the rest of my life—all our lives.

Richard cowered back into the chair. "No, just curious."

~~~~~~~

I couldn't keep my hands still in John Tipton's office. A first visit to a downtown law office was enough to make me bite my nails, something I had given up years before.

"What can I do for you, Mrs. Walker?"

Sitting uneasily opposite John's desk, I took a deep breath. "I want to file for divorce."

"As you may know, there are only two grounds for divorce in this state—adultery and physical cruelty. Which one do you want to use?"

"That's easy. Physical cruelty."

He jotted notes on a legal pad. "Give me some examples." As I recounted a few of the incidents in which Richard had threatened or hurt me, John's eyebrows rose higher and he wrote more notes.

"All right then. It certainly won't be difficult to establish physical cruelty. So let's talk about how to get started. First, we must show that you're no longer living together. Are you living with him now?"

"Yes. In fact, he's at home watching the kids right now." I wondered if John appreciated my satisfaction that Richard was actually helping me to initiate this action.

"Can you get him to move out? I assume you'd like to stay in the house."

I hadn't thought that far ahead yet, and didn't realize he needed to move out so soon. But I wasn't about to back down now. "How soon does he need to be out?"

"He has to be out before we can file."

As much as I feared Richard's reaction to my filing, it seemed that was a reason to act quickly. "I'm in a hurry. I'll get him out soon."

"Good. Let me know as soon as he moves. What about assets?"

"We don't have much. That part should be easy. Part of the problem is he spends so much money when he drinks that we barely get by."

"How much alimony and child support do you want?"

"I won't even insist on alimony. I'd be surprised if he would pay it anyway. He hasn't supported me very well for the last eight years. There's no reason to think he'd do any better after I divorce him. I'll be content if he pays child support. But I don't know what's reasonable."

"Unfortunately, not much. It's based on his earnings. Certainly not enough to actually support the children. The most we can expect is a hundred fifty dollars a month for each child. Are you sure you don't want alimony, too?"

"If I can get it fine, but I won't insist on it. I expect to work. It's the reason I'm going to school. I'm determined to make it—with or without his help."

John buzzed his secretary to bring in several forms for me to sign. He asked me to fill out the forms, but said he couldn't take any action until he heard from me that Richard had moved out. John suggested I try to get him to move out as soon as possible. Perhaps he was afraid if I waited, I'd back down and he would lose a client.

He needn't have worried about me losing my nerve. I walked out of his office feeling strangely warm inside, despite the cloudy, blustery day. I stood for a minute looking up and down the street.

The world should look different somehow. I've just made a huge leap into a different life.

A little rhythmic tune began to run through my head.

I did it, I did it, I really, really did it!

I now faced going back home and persuading Richard to move out—soon.

At least this is a "day after," when he's vulnerable. No better time than the present.

Driving home, I thought about how I would tell him. He had looked so hurt when I told him I was going to see a lawyer. Asking him to move out seemed like twisting a knife in a wound. I resolved to be strong, to resist the puppy-dog looks, the questions, and the pleas for one more chance.

Chapter 29

Changes

"How did it go?" Richard's anxiety showed through his forced smile. My next words wouldn't help.

"It went okay. But there's something I need you to do—and it's a big something."

"What?"

"I need you to move out." I braced for his reaction.

"Oh, come on, Bet. You can't ask me to leave you and the girls. That's not fair."

I took a deep breath and told myself to remain firm. I spoke slowly and deliberately. "Look, Richard, I'm getting the divorce. How difficult it will be is all up to you. One of us will move this week. Either you move, or I move. If I move, that would mean uprooting and upsetting the girls. But if you force me to, that's what I'll do. So which one will it be?"

"Let me think about it for a while."

Sure, take the rest of the day to think about it. Just stay sober.

I saw he didn't like either choice, but I also knew he didn't want to be the bad guy in the eyes of the girls. I just hoped he saw that his moving would be less disruptive for them and, therefore, less likely to cause resentment.

He left to go see his mom, which brought to mind another concern. At times Rita understood my point of view and even protected me to a certain extent. But when it came right down to whether I should stay or leave, her own life was all the testimony I needed to know how she felt. She took "for better or worse, till death do we part" quite literally. Her entire reason for being was to care for, tolerate, and forgive her man, and she expected me to do the same.

I remembered how much she relished the role of martyr. So much so that I sometimes thought part of her was actually grateful for the problematic behavior of Ed and Richard. I remembered how often she bragged about how much she suffered when Richard went missing. I remembered all she did to care for Ed when he was too drunk to care for himself. All in all, she gave up her life for her husband and son.

Mindful of all that, I expected her to resist my decision. I only hoped I could persuade her and Richard that it would be better to go through the process with a minimum of acrimony and dissension.

~~~~~~

Richard returned a couple of hours later with Rita in tow, or maybe it was vice versa.

Oh, no! He's brought her back with him. I need to be strong.

Her back ramrod straight and her head regally erect, Rita walked to the center of the kitchen and stood tall. With Richard beside her, she said, "So, you're going to break your marriage vows, huh, just quit?"

"If you call getting a divorce quitting, then yes, I am. Why don't we sit down? I'll make us coffee."

"None for me, thanks," Rita answered stiffly, but she sat at our small dinette table.

Richard said, "Yeah, I'll have coffee. Sit down, Bet, I'll make it." His saccharine smile gave him a pitiable appearance.

As he made the coffee, Rita continued, "You're just turning your back on your marriage?"

I sat opposite her and tried to think of the best way to answer. Daddy's words popped out of my mouth. "The way I see it, when there's no love left, there's no marriage left."

Uh-oh, did I really say that? I didn't mean to hurt Richard.

"Let me explain." I looked from her to her son, who stood at the sink filling the coffee pot. "Richard, the love I once felt has faded away. I still care for you and I feel sorry for you. I wish you could be better. I even wish I knew how I could help you. But I don't love you anymore with the kind of love a wife should have for her husband. I'm sorry." He didn't turn around. The sudden urgency to thoroughly wash each element of the coffeemaker riveted his attention to the sink.

Rita's face remained stoic. "So you're going to take their daddy away from the girls, too?"

"No. He'll still be able to see them as often as he wants, as long as he's sober. I have no intention of keeping them apart. But I don't want them to be around him when he's drinking. You know how Karen asks to go somewhere else if he's late coming home. She shouldn't have to live in fear of her father. Both of the girls have already seen him drunk far too many times."

Rita didn't attempt to counter my logic. "I don't suppose there's any chance you'll change your mind."

"No, there isn't. I've thought about this for a long time and my mind's made up."

With the coffee finally on, Richard came to sit with us. Muscles in his face quivered slightly and he grasped an empty cup tightly. I did feel pity for him.

But that was all. Pity.

Rita's face didn't soften as much as it settled into defeat. She still didn't look at me directly, but her shoulders relaxed. "Well, if your mind's made up, I don't suppose there's anything I can say to stop you."

I looked at Richard and then back to Rita. "But I do have something to ask. I don't see why we can't get through this peacefully and calmly, like civilized adults. So I'm asking you both, especially for the sake of the children, please don't make this unpleasant."

Richard, still in his day-after state, agreed. Rita's face remained stern, but she nodded.

Richard stood up and took a deep breath. "While I'm waiting for the coffee to brew, I might as well start packing a few things. Do we have any boxes I can use, Trinkatunia?"

"Yeah, I'll get some." I headed out to the storeroom at the end of the carport. As the kitchen door closed behind me, I felt the rush of having cleared another hurdle. I took my time finding the boxes, to give Rita and Richard a few minutes to think about my request—and to quiet my nerves.

I returned with four boxes. "Will these be enough?"

"Thanks, Bet. Yeah, these'll do for now."

He went off to pack, saying, "I'm only taking clothes and personal things for now. I'll come get the big stuff later. Okay?" The politeness sounded strained, but I was grateful for it.

"Yeah, sure. Is there anything I can to do help?"

Ignoring her earlier refusal, I poured coffee for Rita and me. We sat drinking it in stony silence. I remembered when she had regarded me as Richard's hope and her ally. I tried to understand she would naturally be disappointed at me "giving him back." I didn't feel guilty, though. I believed she was the main reason he was the way he was; she deserved to be the one to deal with him from now on.

She had been deep in thought, too, before she finally broke the silence. "You know, I was just thinking about all the money I've spent bailing him out of jams. I can think of more than ten thousand dollars just in the large amounts. There was that first DUI, and the trip to Big Spring, and the trip to Little Rock, and the check for the truck." She paused and sighed. "And of course that doesn't include all the money I've given you because he spent his paycheck. I just don't understand why he doesn't grow up."

For the first time, I worked up the courage to ask a question I wondered if she had ever considered. "Rita, have you ever thought that if you hadn't bailed him out all those times, maybe he would have learned to be more responsible?"

"You sound like Ed. That's what he says, too. But I can't turn my back on my own son. You'll see when it's your own children. You'll help them, too. You'll see."

Right then and there, I made a serious vow to *not* enable such behavior in my children.

Richard's packing finished, he took his boxes to the car, then joined us for coffee. "I'll stay at Mom's temporarily, until I can find a place of my own. I'll come over later to sort through the rest of my things. I only want my personal items. I want you to keep all the household things."

"That's considerate, Richard. Thanks."

Just then Karen came in the kitchen and looked up at me. "Why is Daddy packing his clothes? Is he going on a trip?" Linda was in her room playing, unaware.

I answered, "No, sweetie. Daddy's going to live with Mamaw and Papaw."

"Why?"

Richard cut in, "Mama thinks that'll be better. But I'll miss you and your sister."

"I'll miss you, too, Daddy," she said, then in a lower voice, "...'cept sometimes." Her little face looked worried, afraid of his reaction.

Rita quickly looked away, as if she didn't want to acknowledge Karen's concern.

Richard said, "I know. It's gonna be all right." He reached for her and gave her a hug. Then he quickly turned around and slipped through the back door. As he walked away, his head dropped and his shoulders shook. Rita followed him out, saying nothing, but with her face set in icy disapproval.

After they were gone, Karen asked, "Is Daddy going to live with us anymore?"

"No, sweetheart, he's not."

"Why not?"

"So we don't have to be afraid he might come home drunk."

"Then I'm glad." She climbed into my lap.

"But it means we'll need more money, so I'll have to get a job. You and Linda will have to go to a daycare center."

"What will it be like, Mama?"

"I'm not sure exactly. Except that nice people will take care of you while I'm at work. I'm sure you'll get used to it."

If only I was sure I would get used to it.

Chapter 30
Moving On

When Richard moved out, he took with him our only transportation. I needed a car. My mother took us to several car lots to look at used cars. We settle on a 1967 VW Beetle—only 2 years old and beetle-green. The girls loved the small car, and I loved both the price and the great gas mileage. I had a small sum of money saved, but not enough to cover the cost of the car. Mother lent me the difference, saving me from a car payment. I promised her I would pay it back as soon as I was out of school and earning a living.

I hated my first job almost as much as Linda hated day care. I was a customer service representative for Sears, taking complaint calls. My instructions were to prioritize service calls not in the order received, but according to who screamed the loudest or made the worst threats. Lying to customers and treating them unfairly didn't suit me.

In addition to the job stress, my heart broke each time Linda had to be tugged from my arms in the morning at the day care center. I spent my lunch hour taking Karen from kindergarten to the same center, only to find Linda was crying and begging to go with me. When I returned after work, Linda was still miserable. Karen's adjustment was better than Linda's, but not by much.

Before the end of first week, I was seeking another job and another day care.

By the end of the second week I had found both. Inventory control clerk at a small engineering firm was a better fit for my talents and paid much better. After only two days at the new day care center, Linda liked it so much she was reluctant to leave in the evenings. She and I were both relieved to start and end our days on a happier note.

We soon settled comfortably into a new routine. Even so, the future remained scary. Many evenings after the girls were asleep, I went into the darkened living room, put a record on the stereo, rocked, and cried. And prayed.

Oh, God, I'm so scared. How can I do this alone? How can I raise these two precious girls by myself? I don't see how I can complete my degree, but I don't see what kind of future we'll have if I don't. Please give me guidance and strength.

~~~~~~~

About three weeks after the divorce, I was engrossed in Saturday cleaning when I heard a knock on the back door. On the way to the door, I spotted Richard's truck in the driveway. His slouched, leaning silhouette caused my old fears to stir.

It had been only six weeks since he had come over on Sunday afternoon and taken me with him forcibly, threatening to "degrade me like I had degraded him." With those memories still fresh, I was cautious, but I was also aware I held the cards now.

Before I answered, I pushed the button on the doorknob as I latched the chain. Richard started with, "Lemme in, Bet. I want to see my girls."

The slurred speech confirmed he was drunk. "No, Richard. You've been drinking. I'm not going to open the door with you in that condition."

He shouted, "Yes, you will. I have a right to see my girls."

"No, you don't. You've forgotten we're not married anymore. I don't have to let you in."

"If you don't open this door, I'll break it down."

"If you try, I'll have the police here so fast you won't know what happened." He knocked and threatened again to break down the door.

I went to the wall phone in the kitchen and called the police, deliberately speaking loudly enough for Richard to hear. I had hardly finished the call when I looked out the window and saw him driving away. That was the last time he tried to see me or the girls when he had been drinking.

I was happy to report to the police that he had left and they could cancel the earlier request.

Moran Tank Company designed and manufactured equipment for storing and treating crude oil. My job as inventory control clerk interested me because of my familiarity with this kind of equipment. Most of the contracts were for relatively small items—heaters, treaters, separators, oil storage tanks—destined for the oil fields of Mississippi and Louisiana. But two major contracts were for large, offshore platforms to be shipped down the Mississippi River to the Gulf of Mexico.

When I had been there for just over a month, I was privileged to see the first of these large skids leave our shop. The excitement of moving this large platform the three-quarter mile distance to the river was a momentous event for a company whose entire staff consisted of only ten people in the office and another twenty or so in the shop. All other activity was brought to a standstill as we all stood enthralled at the process.

While we watched the impressive feat, the company's two engineers—John and Ken—explained a little about the function of the equipment. The discussion intrigued me so much that I began to visit with them every chance I got in order to learn more.

I became so fascinated that I considered changing my major from math to engineering, but both John and Ken advised against it. They said the field was male-dominated, and I'd never get a job as an engineer. The best I could hope for would be an assistant at half salary or less. Their advice, coupled with the lack of classes offered at the Resident Center, persuaded me to stick with my plan to teach math. But I still sought every opportunity to learn about engineering from John and Ken.

While I seldom had much money left over after paying bills at the end of the month, I still managed to put a little into savings. Seeing the rewards of my education thus far—I had gotten the job because I had completed two years of school with a concentration in math—gave me great satisfaction. I remembered the nurse's aid job at a hundred seventy dollars a month, only a few years earlier. Now, I earned three hundred seventy-five dollars a month. That might not sound like a lot, even for 1969, but it represented my rise out of poverty and despair. Equally important, I had control of my earnings; I didn't have to worry about an entire paycheck disappearing.

"Mommy, my tooth hurts again." Karen's painful expression tore at my heart. This was the third time in a week she had complained about a toothache. She had not been blessed with strong teeth and I knew she had some cavities, but I was still getting used to my new life—and my new budget. With the demons of insecurity haunting me—I feared the job might disappear unexpectedly—I was reluctant to part with money. But now, Karen's undeniable pain required a trip to a dentist.

The timing couldn't have been more fortunate. I had met Hiram and his wife at the Walkers just a few weeks earlier. They had recently returned to Natchez, where Hiram had opened a dental practice. During their elementary school days, Hiram lived close to the Walkers and he and Richard had become close friends. After the death of his father, when Hiram was only eleven, his mother was left to raise him and his younger brother on a secretary's salary. Hiram and Richard had remained close until high school, when their paths diverged.

I couldn't help noticing the contrast between them. In fact, it was hard to imagine them close friends. Hiram had been focused on becoming a dentist since his early youth, his good grades eventually earning him an academic scholarship. But even with that and a part-time job, he still needed financial help.

Richard, on the other hand, was unencumbered by career ambitions, and admitted he was never much of a scholar. By the time he was in high school, working for his parents gave him enough money for his only interests—cars, boats, and girls.

While they were both about the same height, their builds couldn't have contrasted more sharply. Richard carried a slight hundred fifty pounds on his six-foot-two-inch frame, while Hiram's considerable middle amounted to a more-than-ample weight. Hiram's full, rosy cheeks highlighted the twinkle in his bright gray eyes framed by curly eyelashes.

Perhaps because Ed had seen in Hiram the dedication and ambition so lacking in Richard, he had contributed to Hiram's education. He teased Hiram that he only did it because the family needed a good dentist.

~~~~~~~

"And how are you today, young lady?" Hiram asked Karen, as he helped her into the chair.

Shyly, Karen answered, "My tooth hurts."

"Well, that's what I'm here for. I'm going to make it all better." His tender voice soothed her as he gently patted her hand. "You aren't afraid, are you?"

"A little."

He lowered his voice even more. "I promise I'll try my best not to hurt you. But sometimes we have to make little pricks. Can you be brave?"

"Yes," she answered tentatively.

"Good Girl. Now let's fix that tooth so it won't hurt anymore."

He soon put her at ease and filled the cavity in a short time. Afterward, he gave her a toy and a toothbrush for her bravery, and then wrote a note on her patient information card. He held the card so I could see he had written "paid" on it.

I looked at him and said, "Hiram, I can't— ."

He put his hand up to stop me. "Look, the Walkers have done a lot for me. If it wasn't for their help, I doubt I'd be in this office. Besides, I feel bad you've gotten such a raw deal with Richard. This is something I *want* to do."

"Thank you, Hiram. I truly appreciate this." More than he knew, perhaps. I had made sure I had enough in the bank to cover the visit, but what a relief not to have to write a check.

"You can thank me by bringing her here once a week until we get all her teeth fixed."

"But, I'm not sure—"

Again the hand went up. "Don't say it. Just bring her in every week."

"All right. We'll be here."

On the weekly visits that followed, I found myself responding to Hiram's magnetism as much as Karen. He was both sweet and comical; each visit was more enjoyable than the last.

Toward the end of Karen's last visit, Hiram turned to me. "Well, this does it for Karen. Now, how about if I take a look at your teeth?"

My cheeks flushed. After two pregnancies and years of neglect, I knew there was significant damage. Although I was embarrassed at the prospect of receiving even more free dental care, I knew by then that arguing with him was futile. I took Karen's place in his chair.

"Hmm, look at this, uh-oh, and here, ...and this one needs attention. Okay, I expect to see you in here next week, same time."

"Hiram, you've already—"

"Don't argue. It's the least I can do to support your school effort. Someone helped me get through school, and now I have the opportunity to help someone else. Let me do this for you."

I mock-saluted him. "Yes, sir, I'll be here."

Chapter 31

Hiram

During my first visit to Hiram without Karen, he was more flirtatious than he had been before. It started with, "Velcome to my la-*bor*-atory, my pretty victim...uh, lady." He opened his eyes wide, licked his lips lasciviously, and bared his teeth.

He probably flirts with all his women patients, I thought. Just his personality.

During my second visit, an unmistakable charge filled the air. With a wink, he teased, "Alone again at last." Then with a sweet smile and sincere voice, he said, "You know I look forward to seeing you every week, don't you?" The little voice in my head reminded me he was *married*, but he appealed to a deep-seated need. The temptation to have an adult friend, and especially to have a man notice me as a woman, overpowered any thought of rebuffing his advances. Beside, it was only harmless flirtation.

During the fourth visit, he said, "I go to one or two meetings most weeks, in addition to choir practice. I sure would like to swing by your place afterward. No one would know."

Again, the little voice warned me that what must be hidden and lied about must be wrong. Indeed, the lying itself was wrong. But loneliness overruled my conscience. "Okay, but call first."

"No problem. How about Monday? I have a Dental Society meeting that night. I'll try to get out of there about nine."

This happened on Friday, the day of the standing appointment. Anxiety consumed me all weekend. I didn't know quite what to expect. Even though he had been flirtatious, I still wasn't sure if he simply wanted conversation, or…something more.

Hiding my edginess from the girls on Monday night was difficult. If they were curious why I was more insistent than usual to follow bedtime rules, they didn't let on. At eight forty-five, I was starting to worry they would still be awake when he called. I hovered nervously near their door. By five after nine, I heard the heavy, regular breathing of sleep.

Hiram called at nine fifteen. "Is it okay?" he asked.

"Yes, they're asleep. Come on over."

He parked on a small island situated in a curve about a half block away, a neutral spot not associated with any one house. From the living room window, I watched as he walked, grinning, up the driveway and to the front door. I opened the door just as he reached it to prevent him knocking. I whispered nervously, "Come in, but don't wake the girls."

After he quietly closed the door, he looked down at me and smiled. He reached out for me and slowly drew me to him. With one hand, he pressed my head onto his shoulder. "I've wanted to hold you for so long. And something else I've wanted to do is—" With a finger under my chin, he tilted my face up and pressed his soft lips lightly on mine, then gradually deepened the kiss with smoldering passion. I'd never before been kissed so sensuously. Nerve endings throughout my body sprang to attention. His motives were no longer unclear.

He looked at me again and smiled. "You don't realize how sexy you are, how much you appeal to me, do you? You have no idea how difficult it's been to keep my hands off you in the office."

"I'm not sexy. I'm plain."

"Aw, come on. I find you irresistible. I think your innocence is part of that."

My face was surely the color of a ripe tomato. "You're just saying that."

"Hell, no. Why do you think I'm here? I wouldn't take this kind of chance if I didn't feel a powerful attraction to you."

"Have you ever done this before? Had an affair?"

"Just once. I went to a party alone and a girl came on to me. But it was only one-time. This…, this is a big risk, and I feel guilty about it, I do. But I can't resist you." He pulled me close again. We stood with our arms wrapped around each other, swaying slightly, as if absorbing each other. Even though I couldn't chase away my guilt, neither could I resist the holding, the kissing, or the compliments.

Along with physical appearance and ambition, Hiram's personality contrasted noticeably with Richard's. Hiram's plentiful smiles were warm and welcoming, while Richard's manner was guarded, as if he were holding some part of him inside. Hiram's outlook was cheerful, while Richard was quick to complain and grumble. Hiram's time in college had given him a certain polish and self-assuredness. Richard's time in the local oil fields and bars had done nothing to enhance his social grace.

I suggested we sit in the kitchen and have something to drink. I had made both iced tea and coffee. We chose the coffee.

"Hiram, I'm not sure what we're getting into here. I'm nervous. I've never even thought of doing anything like this."

"I'm nervous, too. All I know is that I find you too appealing to deny. I've watched you grow from a girl into a woman. When we first met, you were shy and insecure. School has given you self-assurance and poise. Even my receptionist has commented on the change in you. As I've watched the transformation, I've come to care for you a lot."

I absorbed the words hungrily. My battered self-worth needed to hear the things he said. I needed to hear that a man found me attractive. I needed to believe I had outgrown the awkward, timorous girl I had been.

"I don't know where this is going, Bettie. Obviously, I can't make you any promises for the future. All I know is that right now, I want to be with you when I can."

"Hiram, don't worry about the future. I'm not even sure of the present, but I enjoy your friendship, and I want to spend time with you, too."

Hiram stood and grasped my hands, lifting me to my feet. Kisses grew passionate, body heat increased, and clothes were unfastened. Suddenly aware of being in the kitchen, with only opaque curtains, we tiptoed down the hall to my bedroom.

Later, after Hiram had gone, I lay basking in the afterglow. I'd never before experienced the kind of sensuous caresses, adoring looks, and sexual attention I had received that evening. For the first time, I could see a difference between merely having sex and making love. I had never questioned whether sex with Richard had been good or not. Since I had nothing to compare it with, I had accepted it as just the way it was. But Hiram had given me a different—and altogether splendid—experience. Not that either of us would have said we were in love, but the attention he gave me was grounded in caring, respect, and a desire to please.

~~~~~

Three more visits to his office completed my dental work, but Hiram's clandestine visits to me continued. He called regularly, even when he couldn't come over. My feelings for him grew stronger than I had intended, even though I knew there was no possibility of a long-term relationship. My pangs of guilt were smoothed over by the much-needed boost to my starved self-esteem.

The confidence I gained from the relationship fostered the hope that if Hiram found me attractive, then maybe someone else would too. Maybe someone waited in my future who would give me all the things Hiram did. Someone single, ready for a long-term relationship. Maybe, just maybe, I wouldn't spend the rest of my life alone after all.

February 1970

I stood looking through the class listings for the spring quarter, hoping a new class might appear magically.

From behind me, I heard Bill Gore's voice. "What are you taking this time?"

"Nothing," I mumbled. "There isn't anything here that I need."

"So what are you going to do?"

I shrugged. "Wait until more classes are offered, I guess."

Bill gestured toward his office. "Come in and have a seat." I followed him into his small office and sat across from him. He leaned back in his chair and frowned as if he were about to interrogate me.

"So how do you plan to finish your degree?"

I had earned about half of the credits required for my bachelor's degree. I shrugged my shoulders. "I don't know. I guess I'll wait and hope for this center to become a four-year school."

"That could be a long time."

"I know, but what other choice do I have?"

"You could move to Hattiesburg and go to school on campus."

"Are you kidding? I can't move to Hattiesburg. I can't afford the move first of all. And even if I could, I can't afford the tuition to go to school full time. Don't forget I have two kids to support."

"I know, I know. Calm down. Have you read the section of the catalog on Student Aid and Scholarships? Or on-campus housing?"

"No, I don't think so."

"Okay. Here's your assignment. Write to the Office of Student Aid and Scholarships and find out what's available, and ask about the Work-Study Program. Next, write to the Office of Student Housing and ask if you qualify for an apartment in the married students housing area, and what the cost is. Let me know what you find out. You've come too far to just stop and wait for something that may never happen."

I knew Bill had a reason for this assignment, so I started working on the letters right away. With no typewriter and my impossible handwriting, it took hours to produce letters that I hoped were legible and reasonably neat. Following tortuous effort, my letters were in the mail.

Two weeks later, I took the responses back to Bill's office.

"Hi, Bettie. What's the good news?"

"Since I'm head of household, I qualify for an apartment in the married students housing complex. The rent's just under $500 a quarter for full-time students. And I'm eligible for a National Defense Student Loan. I'll need to submit a long application, and my mother will have to complete an additional questionnaire. Also, I qualify for the Work-Study Program. I can work up to twenty hours a week."

"Well, let's see what all of this means." Bill asked me a few more questions and we roughed out a tentative budget.

"It'll be close, but I think you can make it, Bettie. Here are all the forms you'll need."

Clutching the batch of paper, I walked out of his office feeling more like a frightened child than a grownup. Moving sounded scary.

What if I move to Hattiesburg and run out of money? What if the classes on campus are harder and I fail? What if the stress of school, work, and taking care of the kids gets to be too much?

I concluded that I wanted my degree badly enough to take the risk. Even though my job was enjoyable enough, it presented no likelihood of advancing beyond clerical worker and the corresponding salary. A degree would bring the potential of a better future for my children and me. By the time I got home, I'd convinced myself to complete the forms.

Coincidentally, Hiram came over that evening. Instead of the usual activities, we sat at my kitchen table and reviewed my school plans. Hiram became my cheerleader, reminding me how hard he had worked to complete school, but also how worthwhile the effort had been. We knew the move would mean the end of our relationship, but then we had known all along it was only temporary.

Chapter 32
The Next Step

Two days after I had finished laying out my plans, Richard came to visit the girls. He had returned to his job for the barge line soon after the divorce, and he had just gotten off the boat for a two-week leave.

"Would you like to come in and have coffee?"

He hesitated before he said, "Sure. What's up?"

I didn't usually ask him in for a visit. "You know how important school is to me, and how much I want to get my degree?"

"Yeah, I know. I'm proud of you for working so hard, Trinkatunia." The tilt of his head and the genuineness of his smile indicated sincerity, at least at that moment.

"I've run out of classes to take here at the Resident Center. I now have two choices. I can stay here, and wait and hope for the remaining courses I need—which could take years—or ... I can move to Hattiesburg and go to school full-time." I watched for his reaction to the second option.

"You're thinking about moving to Hattiesburg?" His eyebrows rose slightly, but he otherwise looked unruffled.

I unveiled the plan. "Bill Gore told me about several programs and housing possibilities. It would be a tight squeeze financially, but if I can depend on you to send child support, I think I can do it. If you remember, the divorce agreement says that if I move out of this house, the amount becomes only a hundred dollars a month, which is less than you're paying now."

Surprisingly, he tilted his head and grinned. "Well, Bet, you won't have to worry about me paying the child support. You can depend on it."

Then his brows knitted. "I just hate to think about the girls being so far away. I won't be able to see them as much."

In reality, since the divorce, he had seen them less and less. He usually saw them when he first came home from the boat, and then he promised to see them more during the two-to three-week stay. But they wouldn't hear from him again until he was about to leave, when he would squeeze in one last visit.

"I know, Richard, but Hattiesburg's only a hundred forty miles away. And you'd be welcome to come get them for the weekend when you're at home. Remember, I promised you I'll never stand in the way of you seeing them, and I intend to honor that."

"I know. Let me think about it, okay?"

"That's fine."

In truth, I didn't need his permission—or even his approval—to move. I had sole custody of the girls, and there were no restrictions against my moving. Nevertheless, it would go smoother for everyone if he agreed. My larger concern was the child support.

~~~~~

"I've been thinking about this all weekend, Bet. I talked to the girls about it. They're excited about the idea of moving, and I know it's a smart thing for you to do. So I won't stand in your way, and I promise I'll send child support." Richard smiled.

I'm amazed he's so agreeable. If only he'll keep his promise...

~~~~~

It took several days to complete the applications: admission as a full-time student on campus, student housing, Work-Study, a couple of scholarships, and—the most crucial one of all—the National

Defense Student Loan. This last one also required a companion form for my mother. On March 26, with crossed fingers, I put them all into the mailbox.

I went home to wait, hope—and pray.

~~~~~~

Though I had worked to get Richard's blessing, I had neglected to put an equal effort into winning Rita over to my side. That oversight turned out to be costly. Since the divorce, she had limited her contact with me to brief chats when visiting with the girls, even though it was I who faithfully took them to see her. Rarely did she come to our house. When we arrived the following weekend, she met us at the car with a stern face and an upright back.

Uh-oh. She's not happy.

"There are my girls." As she turned in their direction, her face instantly softened into a bright smile. "Come on in. I've made cookie dough, and I've been waiting for my helpers to cut out the cookies." Squeals of excitement erupted from Karen and Linda as they scampered out of our Beetle and into her outstretched arms.

When the cookies were in the oven, and the girls had gone out to join Ed on the back patio, she finally spoke directly to me. "So, I hear you're thinking of taking my girls off to Hattiesburg."

Now they were suddenly *her* girls? Her expression had returned to the stern one I had seen at first. "Yes, I'm planning to move. I've taken all the classes offered here, and I really need to finish my degree so I can make a better life for us."

Of course, she had heard all of this before. Although my educational pursuits had seemed harmless enough to her in the beginning, as I had progressed she showed resentment and envy. I believed it stemmed from the fact that she had given up nursing school to marry Ed, and later regretted it. But she would never admit it—that was simply not in her nature.

As if that wasn't enough, now there was a new and different threat. I planned to move her beloved granddaughters away from her. Somehow, I couldn't imagine her driving to Hattiesburg. If she wouldn't drive six miles now, why would she drive a hundred forty miles then? And she knew I wouldn't be able to bring them to her very often.

"Why can't you wait until the Resident Center is expanded?" she asked, her lips pressed tightly together. She knew the answer already.

"Because there is no assurance it will ever happen, and it certainly won't happen soon. Meanwhile, I'm in a dead-end job barely making ends meet. I want something better for us."

"Seems to me you've got it pretty good. I wouldn't mind if someone paid my rent and utilities for me."

Her sarcasm told me she was taking this hard, and the comment about the rent and utilities convinced me it was indeed she who had been paying them. Still, I wasn't prepared for what came next.

"Well, then, if you insist on moving, I'm sure you realize I'll want my furniture back."

What? Her furniture?

"No, I—I didn't," I stammered.

"If you remember, I gave you and Richard the furniture for as long as you lived together. I didn't say anything about it as long as you were still in the same house, but now that you're moving, I'll want it all back."

I don't remember that!

Adrenalin pumped through my body. This was nothing more than pure revenge; her house was filled with furniture much nicer and newer than anything in mine. The used blonde walnut group—living room, dining room, and master bedroom—had been purchased the year Richard and I married. At the time, Rita had called it a wedding present. Nothing was ever said about "as long as you lived together." Later, she had given an old mahogany bedroom set to the girls. This was only because it was in such poor condition, she had cast it off and replaced it.

"And the piano, too. It's Richard's, you know."

As if he is ever going to play it. Why would I think she'd let me keep it? After all, I could use it to earn money, and her grandchildren might play it eventually. Clearly, she's not thinking of the girls' best interest. This is just pure meanness.

Trying to hide how upset I was, I took a couple of deep breaths. I slowly rose and took measured steps out to the back patio.

Ed was apparently not as upset as Rita, because he was calmly playing his "piggy bank" game with the girls, one he had been playing with Karen since she was a toddler. He would put coins in his shirt pocket and have them "find" them. Then they would put them into the large pickle jar he had renamed as the piggy bank. It was a clear jar, enabling them to see the coins add up. They loved hearing the coins plink on the top of the pile.

I patiently waited until they had found all the coins before I used a deliberately restrained voice to say, "Come on, girls. It's time to go."

I turned to Ed. "Sorry to cut this visit short. Rita seems upset."

"Bye, girls." Ed looked at me and shrugged, as if to say he knew but was powerless.

Perhaps Rita thought taking the furniture would cause me to change my mind and stay. Her chances would have been greater had she simply *asked* me to stay. Her attempt to manipulate me only increased my resolve to be independent of Richard and his family.

I'd worked to maintain some kind of agreeable relationship with Rita, but what little that remained broke that day and would never again be made whole.

Chapter 33
Plans Go Awry

Over the next few weeks, the mail brought responses from my letters. First, I received an acceptance letter from Admissions. No surprise there. My grades were good, and I had earned enough credits. Next came approval for the Work-Study Program, again no surprise. I tried not to be let down on learning I didn't qualify for a scholarship, but the student loan was approved. The big disappointment was that, although I was *eligible* for an apartment in married students housing, no apartment was available for the fall quarter. The letter said I would be informed if anything opened up.

Oh, no.

If I couldn't get an apartment on campus, the plan would fall apart. Each element was required, or it simply wouldn't work.

Maybe it's just not meant to be.

When I received notice in early June that an apartment had become available, a thrill ran through me. The final piece had fallen into place. I set a moving date at the end of August. I couldn't wait to tell the two engineers and a couple of other coworkers.

This proved to be unfortunate. The news also traveled to the manager A week later, I was laid off. My boss had heard about my plans and said that since I intended to leave soon, he had decided to go ahead and replace me. Crestfallen, but determined to do the right thing, I set about tidying up my work and writing notes to my successor.

This created a second gap in my financial plans. Not only must I replace the furniture Rita had reclaimed, but now I had also lost over two months' income. At least I could rely on unemployment. Or so I thought.

I received only two unemployment checks when that, too, was terminated. Because of my honesty in reporting my moving plans, I was classified as "unavailable for work." The financial gap widened.

Are unseen forces conspiring against me? Is this a message from somewhere in the universe telling me not to move? NO. I will not accept that.

I refused to panic. Not yet. I needed that degree. I remembered one more potential source of money. . .

~~~~~~~

"Hey, Mom, remember that life insurance policy you took out on me a long time ago?"

"Yes, why do you ask?"

"I've just lost my unemployment compensation. So now, in addition to buying furniture and moving, I need money to live on for six weeks. I have a little saved, but not enough for all that."

"Well, I guess it must have accumulated some value. But I hate to cash it in."

A couple of days later, Mother came over with the policy. We read it together and concluded it had a value of about $736.00. A call to the company confirmed this and explained how to turn it in.

Mother was hesitant. "I've always thought the only reason I'd cash this in would be an emergency."

"As far as I'm concerned, this is an emergency. Without this money, I can't move and I'll be stuck here."

She thought about it for a few minutes, then relented. She sent a request and a couple of weeks later, we had a check.

Right before moving day, Hiram came over one last time. He couldn't stay long. We sat in the living room, drinking tea and rehashing my plans. Like a big brother, he issued advice and encouragement. "Now, you study hard, you hear? No matter how tough it is, don't give up. Promise me?"

"I promise. Believe me, I'm not about to give up now."

He put his arm around my shoulder and pulled me close. "I'll think about you and miss you. It'll be hard to arrange, but I'll try to get over to see you."

It wasn't likely he would actually come to Hattiesburg, but I knew I'd be coming back to Natchez occasionally. "May I drop by to see you when I'm back in town?"

"I'd be hurt if you didn't. Now, go get 'em, kid."

On a Monday in late August, we left Natchez early in the morning. Mother towed a fully-loaded cargo trailer with her Oldsmobile, and I followed in my packed VW Beetle. Karen rode with Mother and Linda rode with me. We reached Hattiesburg before noon and soon located Pine Haven, the cluster of on-campus apartments for married students and families. A quick trip to the office, with paperwork in hand, produced keys and an apartment number.

Each building held eight apartments—two on each side upstairs and two on each side downstairs. In the center of each building were large, central breezeways, great places for the adults to socialize and for the kids to play. We were in Building O, apartment 203, upstairs in the right rear.

The sturdy block construction had allowed the old buildings to survive well. The interiors could generously be described as efficiently designed—or more to the point, compact. The front door opened directly into the living room, with an eating area and narrow kitchen on the right. A short hall led to a bathroom hardly bigger than my outstretched arms and two petite bedrooms.

By afternoon's end, we had emptied the trailer, including my portable dishwasher. I refused to leave it behind. Rita had taken a lot from me, but that was one thing she had no right to. I wasn't sure what I'd do with it if I couldn't use it, but I wouldn't leave it behind. Fortunately, it fit into the corner of the eating area.

The next test was to see if it could actually be used. It barely fit into the narrow space in front of the sink, and when it was hooked up to the faucet, it blocked access to most of the kitchen. But it worked!

Because the apartment was cramped, in disarray, and hot—there was no air conditioning—Mother headed back home as soon as we unloaded and dropped off the trailer.

Shortly before the move, I had bought used furniture to replace the pieces Rita had reclaimed. A few hand-me-down pieces from my mother filled a few spaces.

Before I knew *how* small the girls' bedroom would be, I had bought twin beds and a small, used dresser. But their room was so small that with both beds set up in their new room, there wasn't enough space to open the dresser drawers. They decided they would rather share one twin bed and have more space. Being skinny had its advantages.

My double bed and dresser filled my room, too, with no space for the chest. Fortunately, the closet had no doors, but was simply a recessed area with a clothes rod and shelf above it. This allowed me to tuck the chest into one end of the closet. My few clothes didn't require the entire length of the hanging space anyway. To round out our furnishings, I picked up a few used tables for the living room that departing students had discarded.

Even though we were cramped, I had no complaints. I had lived in circumstances far worse.

Within a few days, the girls and I had settled in and made friends with the neighbors. Karen and Linda were happy to discover several other children near their ages in the building. I was happy that one of the neighbors was a single mom. All the other residents made us feel welcome.

Only one thing disturbed our comfort—the heat. Because the buildings had no air conditioning, most people had window units. But money was much scarcer than I had originally planned, and I didn't have enough to buy an air conditioner yet. I had hoped to get by with only a fan for the few remaining weeks of fall. September might be autumn on the calendar, but the thermometer still read summer.

Mid-September brought an intense heat wave, with highs in the upper nineties and lows in the mid-eighties. Open windows were useless because there wasn't even the slightest breeze. The humidity hung at ninety percent or greater. It was, as Daddy would have described it, "close," as if the air itself was trying to suffocate us. None of us could sleep at night without the fan, and there was no way to position it to blow into both bedrooms at once. So the three of us piled into my bed until late October brought cooler temperatures.

Child care turned out to be easier in Hattiesburg than it had been in Natchez. Soon after registration, several of us in our building compared notes and figured out how we could trade babysitting in the evenings so that none of us had to part with precious money. And for daytime, I found a neighbor who lived two buildings away to watch Linda all day and Karen after school.

Meanwhile, I was filled with ambition with I registered for classes, choosing five. Four met during the day and the fifth at night. I also worked the maximum twenty hours each week. Daytime classes were either Monday-Wednesday-Friday or Tuesday-Thursday. I had two of each of these. The night class met only one night per week from six-thirty to ten.

For that first quarter, my weekday classes were all in the afternoon, and I worked each day from eight until noon to make the twenty hours.

I soon realized why I should not have classes soon after lunch. Nearly always sleep-deprived, I struggled to stay awake during those early afternoon classes. I used every tactic I knew of—taking deep breaths, pinching myself, and thinking of something exciting.

It was a difficult quarter, but I made it through—and with decent grades.

My work-study job was for the Department of Education in the College of Education and Psychology. I was one of six students assigned to the full-time secretary, Catherine Jabour, a short, round, always-smiling mother hen to us students. To this day I can't think of her without seeing her face crinkled into a warm smile.

Since we typed and duplicated class materials for the eight professors in the group, often needed on short notice, she preferred having help in the morning most days. But Mrs. Jabour also needed someone to work Friday afternoons for important end-of-week tasks. Few other students wanted to work Friday afternoon, though, because they wanted to either party Friday night or go home for the weekend.

Beginning with my second quarter on campus, I arranged all my classes in the mornings, when I was fresher, and work in the afternoons, which meant I was there on Friday afternoon. Mrs. Jabour appreciated the trade-off.

The only almost-fatal flaw in my planning was time for sleep, or lack thereof. My new schedule didn't permit the seven to eight hours I needed. Not even close. I had to be up at six thirty to get the girls to the neighbor's by seven thirty and be in class by eight. Karen went to school from the neighbor's. Even though I picked up the girls by four thirty or five, my day wasn't nearly over.

My night class met from six thirty to ten, so on that night I had little more than an hour to make dinner and feed the girls before I had to leave for class. The other evenings, after dinner and before the girls' bedtime, I typed papers for other students. The seventy-five cents a page was grocery money. Study time came after the girls were asleep. Often, I was up until one or two in the morning. Six thirty came too soon.

As if I didn't have enough packed into my schedule, I maintained my routine church involvement: choir practice on Wednesday nights and church services on Sunday mornings.

By Friday afternoon, I was operating on depleted energy to the point that I was past tired, running only on nervous energy. In addition, one of my Friday afternoon tasks was to thin all the bottles of Liquid Paper. We used quite a bit of the correction fluid, and the bottles and brushes got caked by the end of the week. The thinner for the Liquid Paper contained toluene. I didn't know at the time that is was sometimes used as a recreational inhalant, but I was aware that I seemed to be in a lighthearted mood by the time all the bottles of Liquid Paper were ready for the next week.

Friday evening, when I was bone-tired but curiously peppy, became the time in the weekly routine for what little cleaning got done. The physical activity helped me to unwind, and then I usually slept as if I were drugged.

When early-bird Linda awoke on Saturday mornings, usually around seven or eight, she wanted me awake, too. She tried to rouse me from my stupor by poking me in the eyes, saying, "Mommy, Ope' your eyes. Wake up. Ope' your eyes, Mommy." Her soft little finger raised my eyelids to force me awake.

The most I managed was to mumble, "Go have some cereal and watch cartoons." Not exactly mother-of-the-year behavior, but the best I could muster.

By around ten, I'd drag myself out of bed and start on tasks that couldn't be done during the week: grocery shopping; maybe taking the girls to the park, the zoo, or a movie. Later in the day, I sewed. Making some of our clothes was another way of staying within our pitifully small budget.

It was as if I started my week by stepping onto a slow-moving merry-go-round. Each day the speed increased until on Friday night, I was slung off and allowed the weekend to recover from the dizziness. There never seemed to be enough time to get everything done.

One thing that didn't occupy my time was trips to the bank to deposit checks from Richard.

None had come.

Chapter 34
More Angels

November 1970

I had called Richard over several weeks. Each time, Rita's icy voice replied, "Richard's on the river. I'll talk to him when he comes home."

My lack of money drove me to call John Tipton, my divorce attorney. "John, Richard hasn't sent any money since I moved. Every time I call, his mother says he's on the river."

John said, "Well, let's see, you moved at the end of August, so he owes for September, October, and November?"

"Yes, three months."

"I'll see what I can do."

Two weeks later, I received a letter from John in which he apologized for his lack of progress. He had met with the same resistance I had. Every time he called either Richard's mother or Canal Barge Line, he was told Richard was on the river. The Mississippi River is federal waters and doesn't come under the jurisdiction of any state, so Richard was virtually untouchable. John said he would keep trying, but not to expect much.

He included his bill.

Great, no more money coming in, but more money going out. Not exactly what I was going for.

Without the child support, I tried to find more typing jobs. From after dinner until late into the evening, I typed papers for other students. My own assignments often had to wait. More than a few nights, I awoke at two or three in the morning, my head on the typewriter, my hand imprinted on my forehead, with no recollection of having stopped typing. And no homework done.

I learned to make use of even small amounts of time between classes for assignments. I started smoking again, remembering how that had seemed to keep Rita alert. I also discovered NoDoz.

A check from Richard in early December was a surprise, but it was only for one month—a hundred dollars. It was better than nothing, but John's fee took half of it. With Christmas approaching, I barely had enough money for Hamburger Helper and macaroni and cheese.

Where will I get money for Christmas? These girls are too young to be disappointed on Christmas morning.

I hinted to Mother, but she responded that she knew how much I wanted to be independent. I never worked up the courage to ask her why she so willingly financed my older brother through his bachelor's degree—and then through graduate school to earn his doctorate—while she was so reluctant to help me.

Maybe it was a mistake to move to Hattiesburg and commit us to such a tight budget. My education is important, but at what price?

~~~~~~

"Mama, how many days till Christmas now?" For the last week, Linda had been asking at least once a day.

"Fifteen," I sighed. Oh, how I wished we could skip Christmas this year.

"Just two weeks, right?" asked Karen.

"Just about."

Please, I thought, someone give me more typing, or these kids won't have a Christmas.

I had barely enough money for us to eat, certainly not enough to buy presents for my daughters. At five and seven, Linda and Karen were young enough to wholeheartedly believe in Santa, yet old enough that they would remember if he disappointed them this year. If I didn't get a couple of jobs soon, I didn't know what I'd do.

I cringed at the thought of my children waking up Christmas morning to find nearly nothing under the tree. An unbearable scene unfolded in my head:

"Crayons? That's all Santa brought? But I was a good girl..."

"Socks? Santa's supposed to bring toys, not socks."

"Why doesn't Santa like us?"

Ten days before Christmas, we found a Charlie Brown–like spruce at the edge of a tree lot that the owner let me have for nearly nothing. We proudly took it home and put our hand-me-down and homemade decorations on it. Karen and Linda were crossing off the days on our wall calendar.

But I still had no money. Three more days went by with no typing jobs—no phone calls or knocks on the door. I should have realized that students wouldn't need any papers typed so near the holidays.

I went to my work-study job on the last day before the break, now just one week before Christmas. One of my duties was to get the mail at the campus post office. I didn't mind, and while there, I usually checked my own. I was surprised to see several pieces standing behind the window of the box.

The return address on one envelope was that of my long-time friend Susan, and on the second that of my Uncle Howard. Probably Christmas cards. But there was no return address on the third. Although curious, I was in a hurry and decided to open them later.

I trudged back to the office and delivered the mail. After I'd made test copies for one professor and typed five more pages for another, Mrs. Jabour said, "Go home. No one will care if you leave early. Go have a merry Christmas with your girls."

I put on the jolliest face I could muster as I returned the good wishes and thanked her for letting me leave early. With no hope for any more income in the next week, I was quite uncertain about the "merry" part.

Outside the office, I remembered the mail. I opened the first two envelopes while I walked toward our small apartment. They were thoughtful Christmas cards, but not unexpected. The third one piqued my curiosity. I slowly lifted the flap of the envelope and discovered that it, too, was a Christmas card. The message inside was printed in scrawled capital letters and said simply, "MERRY CHRISTMAS FROM SANTA."

But who is this from? Odd.

As I started to put the card back in the envelope, I noticed something else in the envelope. It was a Sears gift certificate for one hundred dollars.

I had to sit down. Someone had become my very own Christmas angel!

Plopped on a low wall, I wiped the tears that involuntarily trickled down my cheeks. Who sent this? Who knew how desperate I was? My mind searched to try to figure out who had sent the card. Could it have been Mrs. Jabour? Or maybe it was Dr. Peterson, the department chairman. He had been very encouraging to me. Or perhaps Dr. Wallace. She was the only female professor in the department and had been a single mother when she was in graduate school.

Suddenly, I realized I had something more urgent to think about than trying to solve the puzzle. I needed to arrange for the girls to stay with a neighbor while I made a trip to Sears. I only hoped our local store still had the Hot Wheels that Linda had her heart set on and the life-size baby doll that Karen longed for.

After rushing home, I went next door and whispered my good fortune to my neighbor Rosemary. She was such a good friend I might have suspected the card came from her except that she and Lester were nearly as poor as I was. Although they certainly didn't have an extra hundred dollars to spare, she graciously offered to watch the girls for me.

~~~~~

"Oh, look, Karen," Linda shouted. "Santa came last night! He brought me the Hot Wheels."

"Yay! Come on, Mama. Look what Santa brought. He left me a big baby doll." The girls were gleefully ripping paper off boxes before I even got to the living room.

I wondered if there was any sweeter sound in the world than happy, excited children on Christmas morning. I whispered a heartfelt thank-you to my anonymous donor. One more time God had answered my prayer using humans as angels.

When I returned to school and work after the holidays, I broadcast my appreciation to everyone I knew, hoping the message would find its way to my angel-Santa. And I read into that gift a sign—a sign I was doing the right thing after all. At least one other person agreed with me.

Because I had not received any child support since the one check in December, I contacted John Tipton in March. One more check appeared in May—again for only one month. I also received a letter from John saying he didn't believe it was cost-effective to me for him to continue the fight on my behalf. He enclosed contact information for the Secretary of State along with the suggestion I continue the effort on my own.

A few days later I mailed my first letter to the Secretary of State in Jackson.

On a Tuesday in late May, Richard called to tell me that his father had passed away and the funeral was to be on Friday morning. He seemed to expect me to rush right back to Natchez and attend the funeral. He was disappointed when I told him I would not miss class or work on Friday, but that I would bring the girls over on Saturday.

I felt it was my duty to honor the relationship between the girls and their grandmother, so I dropped off the girls early Saturday afternoon. Because I didn't want to spend much time with Rita, I drove over to my mother's for the night. I returned for the girls on Sunday afternoon.

Just as we were getting ready to leave, Karen innocently asked her grandmother if she could take her piggy bank. She, of course, referred to the large pickle jar that she and her grandpa had filled with coins. He had started playing a game with her since she was little more than a year old. He would invite her to reach into his shirt pocket to see what was in there. Sometimes it would be candy, but often it was change. Of course, she ate the candy, but he urged her to put the coins in a large pickle jar, telling her she could buy lots of candy one day. She had fun hearing the coins clink.

With Grandpa now gone, she wanted the promised money.

Rita looked at me sharply as she answered Karen, "No, you can't have it. Your mother would just take it from you and spend all the money."

I can't believe she hates me so much she's taking it out on Karen. What have I ever done to make her think I'd steal from my own child?

Karen's face was crestfallen. When Rita tried to hug her goodbye, Karen's little body stiffened. On that day, Karen's warm attachment to her grandmother turned into cool caution.

I remembered how wounded I felt when Rita announced she was taking back the furniture. Now, she was "taking back" the coins Karen had been told were hers.

Was there no end to this woman's cruelty?

December 1971

Six months of correspondence back and forth to the Secretary of State failed to yield results, so I gave up the fight to collect child support from Richard. I promised myself I would resume it later, although I never did.

The frenetic pace of school and work led to a lack of sleep, which lowered my resistance so that every bug that came along took hold, or so it seemed. Then, of course, I passed it on to the kids—or I got it from them. We traded strep throat, bronchitis, intestinal flu, and anything else that came around. I didn't have enough stamina to take on more typing than I was already doing. And there wasn't any other way to earn extra money. I was already working the maximum twenty hours a week allowed on my work-study program.

With another Christmas approaching, I faced the same dilemma as the year before. Where could I find money for Christmas? I tried not to worry about it as much this time, hoping a solution would appear. I knew by then to not hope for any help from my mother. But as the date grew closer, I couldn't help feeling anxious.

Once again, an anonymous donor came to the rescue. Three unexpected envelopes with no return addresses appeared in the mail. This time we received three separate Christmas cards. Each card contained money—twenty-five dollars each for the girls and fifty-dollars in mine. No name on the cards, only a printed "SANTA."

Thank you, God, for sending me another angel.

February 1972

"Mommy, my tooth hurts." This time it came from Linda. Driving back to Natchez to see Hiram was out of the question.

Where, oh where can I find the money for an extra expense?

But I had no choice. She needed to see a dentist right away. I prayed for another miracle as I made an appointment with someone local.

"I can fill the cavities in two more visits, but she needs to see an orthodontist right away to make room for her permanent teeth." Dr. Palmer had finished his initial examination. I knew Linda's teeth were crowded and that braces would be needed eventually, but I was surprised he recommended seeing an orthodontist at only seven years old. I was already struggling to figure out how to pay for having a few cavities filled. How could I possibly afford an orthodontist?

Dr. Palmer added, "By the way, I see you're a student at Southern. I remember what it was like when I was in school, so I have a special rate for students." He smiled and winked as he explained he would charge me only half the normal fee.

Only half? What a relief! I'm not sure he knew how much that meant. The lower amount was still a strain to the budget, but *much* better than the original amount.

Then he asked, "Would you like me to recommend an orthodontist?"

"Yes, please do. And thank you so much for the reduced rate. I'm not sure how I'm going to pay you, but I'll figure out something." I hope I thanked him enough.

"I'm not worried. You can take your time."

Should I spend this much money? Will it make a difference next week? Will it make a difference next year? Will it make a difference in five years?

These questions had become my test for whether to spend money. The five-year test was, of course, the highest priority. The orthodontist certainly passed the five-year test. But where could I find the money?

I even considered swallowing my pride and begging Rita to persuade Richard to pay the child support he owed. I thought a request on behalf of Linda's teeth might carry some weight, but I had little hope I'd actually get any money from him. By now, Richard only called when he was drunk. He made big promises to come see the girls and to send money, but he never did either.

Also, Rita hadn't called in months—not since Ed passed away. Her contact with Karen and Linda had tapered after we moved to Hattiesburg, but I thought she might want more contact with the girls after Ed's passing, even after the piggy-bank incident.

"Mama, why doesn't Grandma Rita call us anymore?" Linda asked.

"I don't know, sweetie. Maybe she's busy."

"I miss making cookies with her and I miss seeing Grandpa Ed."

Karen had seldom mentioned her grandmother since the piggy bank, so I was not surprised at her reaction. "I miss Grandpa Ed, too. But I think Grandma Rita doesn't like us anymore."

What do I say now?

"I'm sure she still loves you, honey."

But if she does, she sure has a peculiar way of showing it.

Not that I was eager for Rita to spend more time with my daughters, but it hurt me that she ignored them and made them sad.

I concluded that if she didn't care about them enough to call, she wouldn't be willing to send money.

I saw only one way to get the money for Linda's treatment. I was wary about misusing credit, but I had started receiving credit card offers in the mail. For the sake of Linda's teeth, I got a cash advance from one of the offered cards.

The orthodontist fit Linda with a headgear to be worn ten hours a day, her first step in preparation for braces. She didn't mind wearing it, except for the tenderness it caused. And the orthodontist was as flexible as the dentist had been about the payment, thank goodness.

Neither of them worked for free, though. One thing was clear. Expenses were increasing. But I had only two more quarters of school to go.

If I can just find a way to survive a little longer...

Chapter 35
My Moment

In January, I received an unexpected letter from my older half-brother, Lester, telling me that he was proud of my effort in school. He said he had intended to contribute to my tuition for months, and apologized for not sending something sooner. He also apologized it couldn't be more than the amount he enclosed.

It was five hundred dollars! It seemed like a million dollars. With that, I could survive for another few months. Another angel.

~~~~~~

Even though I was tired all the time, and had to watch every penny I spent, I could see the end in sight. I still had one more difficult math class and I needed another elective. I was pursuing a Bachelor of Science instead of a Bachelor of Arts partly because of the difference in the language requirements. A B.S. only required one foreign language class. Computer programming was still in its infancy, and most schools were encouraging students toward that field. USM had recently established a new policy that computer science counted as a foreign language.

All that lead me to take Introduction to FORTRAN as my last elective. FORTRAN was the most frequently used coding language at that time, and the one most students started with. It also seemed to complement my math degree. Years later, I would be grateful for that decision. That one class help me get a great job.

It was frustrating and fun at the same time. Writing good code required much trial and error, which made it time-consuming. I spent a lot of time in the programming lab, typing stacks of card decks and handing them in to the computer operator and waiting for the output. When the code finally worked, it was extremely rewarding.

But I was also struggling with that hard math class, which required extra study time. I even sought out a couple of other students to study with, something I rarely did.

I got even less sleep than ever that last quarter. The payoff was in sight, though, and I had to figure out a way to make it a just few more weeks. While I waited for grades to be posted, I was as nervous and I'd been taking those first few classes and wondering if I could actually pass college classes.

When I discovered that I not only passed, but with decent grades, I let out a big sigh. I had done it. It hadn't been easy and certainly hadn't been pretty, but it looked like I would finally get my degree. All that remained was filling out the paperwork and get it approved.

June 1972

As I sat in the midst of hundreds of other graduates, listening to speeches and then the seemingly endless list of names, as students paraded across the stage to receive diplomas, many thoughts occupied my mind.

Would anyone here believe me if I described how, only a few years ago, I was living in a dilapidated mobile home in a cow pasture, doing laundry by hand outside, and crawling through a barbed wire fence to come and go? Would I have believed it if someone had told me then that I would be receiving a diploma on this night?

But I *had* made it. Not alone, though. I thought of the many people who had contributed to my achievement, without whom I doubt I would have been sitting there.

I thought of Jerry, whose counsel and encouragement guided me out of despair, through anger, and to determination. And Sharon, my classmate, who helped me understand a child's view of alcoholism. Also Virginia and Pauline at Al-Anon, who gave me clarity about my marriage by showing me what my choices were.

Hmm, the graduate degrees have all been awarded. Now they're starting on the College of Science.

Hiram boosted my ego and strengthened my resolve when I needed it most. Bill Gore encouraged and challenged me and led me to Hattiesburg. Mrs. Jabour helped me keep my chin up and my eyelids open on after only four hours of sleep. And, of course, my two anonymous Santas, who not only helped my children have nicer holidays, but inspired me to resolve do something similar for others. More recently, my brother Lester's generosity helped me make it to the finish line.

Oh, College of Science is finished. They've started on my college—Education and Psychology.

My thoughts turned to Richard. As far as I knew, he was still drinking and still irresponsible. I wondered what he would think if he could see me now. If he were sober, he'd probably be proud, but envious. If not, he'd make fun of me, and surely call me "Little Miss Perfect."

But I didn't need his approval. Not anymore.

I need to pay attention to the alphabet now. They're on the M's.

Nor did I need Rita's approval. She had virtually written me out of her life. Her initiative to see, or even talk to, the girls had faded away. Remembering how, only a few years earlier, she had been so attached to them, I was appalled she ignored them now. Her resentment and anger toward me had apparently spilled over to them, too. How could she not see that what I had accomplished was worthwhile for them and for me?

Oh, I heard a W.

An usher came to the end of my row and gestured for us to rise and start toward the dais. As I exited my row and approached the platform, some of those in front of me appeared bored. But I knew there must be others for whom this night marked the culmination of a long and arduous effort. Only a few steps away from the podium, I heard my name. "Bettie Wailes Walker." As I covered the short distance, I wanted time to stop time so I could capture the moment.

After almost six years of study, hard work, and determination, I had made it! I wanted to shout to the world, "This is my moment."

As I moved the tassel from the right side of the mortar board to the left, and exited the other side of the dais, I was aware of the same sort of conflicting emotions I had felt walking out of the courthouse in Natchez three years earlier. I was relieved it was over, and proud of my persistence and strength. At the same time, I was afraid of going out into the world.

School had been a protective cocoon where I only needed to think about life in three-month segments—just make it through the current quarter. But now the time had come to apply my knowledge and experience.

However, I felt proud that I had prepared myself to earn a living, and to finish raising my daughters, who were becoming more complex by the year. With a combination of eagerness and trepidation I wondered what the next chapter in our lives would be. I knew one thing for certain. Whatever lay ahead for us, it promised to be better than our past.

I'll never live in a cow pasture again!

Epilogue

After graduation, I stayed in Hattiesburg and taught at a nearby high school for one year. I took graduate classes at night, and planned to complete my Master's degree. In June, I returned to school full-time. However, my expenses went up more than expected. Both Karen and Linda needed dental work again, and Linda's orthodontic treatment continued. With most other costs increasing, too, I found my credit card debt growing each month. By the beginning of winter quarter, with eroded energy, mounting debt, and Christmas approaching, I realized I couldn't afford to stay in school. I decided to withdraw from school and find a teaching job.

A visit to the placement bureau revealed several openings in Florida. The week before Christmas, we made a hurried trip that included three job interviews in Orlando. In each case, I was told there was a ninety percent chance of getting the job. Pretty good odds, even to a math major.

We spent the week following Christmas packing. On January 3, having withdrawn from school, we struck out for Orlando, me driving a huge U-Haul truck with the green Beetle trailing behind on a tow-bar—a story that could fill another book. Within two weeks, I was teaching math at Apopka High School, a suburb of Orlando.

A year and a half later, as a result of a severe recession in the state, I was laid off.

How could this happen? I worked so hard to have a secure job, and now this?

I floundered for another year, living on a scary edge financially, before landing a job at Martin Marietta as a software engineer.

The last year I taught, my contract was for slightly over eight thousand dollars a year, and my starting salary at Martin was almost fourteen thousand dollars a year. Quite a difference. Yes, way back in the cow pasture, I had gotten it right after all. Education was the answer.

Among my several assignments at Martin was one in the area of simulation—specifically, aircraft simulators. That's where I found a niche into which I seemed to fit naturally. I went on to have a long career as a software engineer at small companies, developing software for simulation and training devices.

~~~~~~~

I've come a long, long way from the fifteen-year-old girl willing to settle for the first boy to come along, and whose life spiraled downward into an abyss of despair and hopelessness. Occasionally, when someone describes me as "self-assured" or "strong," I grin inside, remembering how I was back then. Would I change my past? No. First, I know for a certainty there is no one else I can blame for anything that happened to me. Not my parents, not Richard. No one but me made the choices that led to the difficulties I experienced. Everything that happened did so because I chose it or allowed it.

Second, those very experiences molded me into who I am today. Easy times rarely build character, develop strength, or provide opportunities to overcome challenges. Difficult, trying times offer us opportunities to find what we're made of. In a strange way, I'm grateful for every unpleasant day, every moment of despair, every trial. Because of what I've endured and conquered, I know I'm strong. I can survive whatever may come.

~~~~~~~

Even though I had a few serious relationships over the years, I never remarried. The last of those relationships ended with his death in 1994. By that time, I had become a marathon runner, and spent nearly all of my time either working or running.

Then in 2003, I made a career change and started a tutoring center, returning to my original goal of teaching math. Between running and managing a business, when would I have time to develop a relationship? I didn't expect to find anyone at my then-advanced age.

But in 2013, the man of my dreams found me. Jim is the man I fantasized about way back during my marriage, when I wished Richard could just be nice, honest, and decent.

My sweetheart is all of those things and more. He is sweet, honorable, romantic, and humorous—all the things I wished Richard had been.

At last, I have the love of my life.

www.ingramcontent.com/pod-product-compliance
Lightning Source LLC
Chambersburg PA
CBHW031441040426
42444CB00007B/916